Cambridge Elements ≡

Elements in Shakespeare and Pedagogy
edited by
Liam E. Semler
University of Sydney
Gillian Woods
Birkbeck College, University of London

PODCASTS AND FEMINIST SHAKESPEARE PEDAGOGY

Varsha Panjwani
New York University, London

T0349857

CAMBRIDGE
UNIVERSITY PRESS

Shaftesbury Road, Cambridge CB2 8EA, United Kingdom

One Liberty Plaza, 20th Floor, New York, NY 10006, USA

477 Williamstown Road, Port Melbourne, VIC 3207, Australia

314–321, 3rd Floor, Plot 3, Splendor Forum, Jasola District Centre,
New Delhi – 110025, India

103 Penang Road, #05–06/07, Visioncrest Commercial, Singapore 238467

Cambridge University Press is part of Cambridge University Press & Assessment,
a department of the University of Cambridge.

We share the University's mission to contribute to society through the pursuit of
education, learning and research at the highest international levels of excellence.

www.cambridge.org
Information on this title: www.cambridge.org/9781108977180

DOI: 10.1017/9781108973311

First published 2022

A catalogue record for this publication is available from the British Library.

ISBN 978-1-108-97718-0 Paperback
ISSN 2632-816X (online)
ISSN 2632-8151 (print)

Additional resources for this publication at www.cambridge.org/panjwani.

Podcasts and Feminist Shakespeare Pedagogy

Elements in Shakespeare and Pedagogy

DOI: 10.1017/9781108973311
First published online: October 2022

Varsha Panjwani

New York University, London

Author for correspondence: Varsha Panjwani, vp46@nyu.edu

ABSTRACT: Scores of women feel excluded from Shakespeare Studies because the sound of this field (whether it is academics giving papers at conferences or actors sharing performance insights) is predominantly male. In contrast, women are well represented in Shakespeare podcasts. Noting this trend, this Element envisions and urges a feminist 'podagogy' which entails utilizing podcasts for feminism in Shakespeare pedagogy. Through detailed case studies of teaching women characters in *Hamlet*, *A Winter's Tale*, *The Merchant of Venice*, and *As You Like It*, and through road-tested assignments and activities, this Element explains how educators can harness the functionalities of podcasts, such as amplification, archiving, and community building to shape a Shakespeare pedagogy that is empowering for women. More broadly, it advocates paying greater attention to the intersection of Digital Humanities and anti-racist feminism in Shakespeare Studies.

KEYWORDS: Shakespeare, podcasts, feminism, pedagogy, Digital Humanities

ISBNs: 9781108977180 (PB), 9781108973311 (OC)
ISSNs: 2632-816X (online), 2632-8151 (print)

Contents

Introduction: Firewalls and Activisms

In summer 2019, we found a room of our own. By 'we', I mean a group of seven Shakespeare students and me, their Shakespeare lecturer. The nexus of our identities is far more complex than the terms 'Shakespeare students' or 'Shakespeare lecturer' suggest because we are not defined by Shakespeare alone. I am a Shakespeare scholar and a woman of colour and a feminist teacher. The students are also scholars in various disciplines, including Shakespeare, and they are Black, Asian, and White women and men, some of whom identify as queer. This diversity is important to us and is something that we carry into our work. The room we found and founded was a digital room or, more specifically, it was a podcast. A podcast is a series of digital audio files (most commonly in MP3 or .wav format) that are distributed over the Internet using syndication, and it is also a space where these audio files are deposited online for subsequent asynchronous consumption. Thus, it can be understood both as an audio broadcast that listeners can subscribe and listen to as soon as it is released and a digital room where such audio files are collected to be enjoyed at leisure. We chose a podcast because we wanted to utilize both these properties that this medium-cum-space enables. In *A Room of One's Own*, Virginia Woolf (1929) insists that women need a room for imaginative thinking and writing, and they require access to works by other women so that they can take courage from their predecessors. Through the podcast, we sought to create such a space within Shakespeare Studies which would both broadcast and store a range of women's thoughts and voices. Therefore, the *Women & Shakespeare* podcast, which is now in its third series, features conversations with diverse women creatives and academics who are involved in making and interpreting Shakespeare.[1] We are not alone in this podcast universe or 'podverse' because, as Section 1 details, many Shakespeare podcasts are either created or hosted by or regularly feature women critics and practitioners (thereby

---

[1] www.womenandshakespeare.com. Deepest thanks to NYU for the Global Faculty Fund Award which financed the first series and to David Monteith – the best podcasting teacher ever.

emphasizing their scholarship and experience).[2] In our collective desire to harness a podcast for gender equity, such Shakespeare podcasts can claim kinship with cyberfeminist academics, theorists, educators, practitioners, and activists who, as Jessie Daniels (2009) summarizes, have proved that '[i]nternet technologies can be an effective medium for resisting repressive gender regimes' (101). Owing to this close alliance, this Element argues that podcasting technology is already playing or has the potential to play an important role in shaping a Shakespeare pedagogy that is empowering for women. In other words, this Element both envisions and analyses a feminist Shakespeare 'podagogy'.

The term 'podagogy' is already in circulation; a slew of podcasts include the word in their names. For instance, *Podagogies* is hosted by Chelsea Temple Jones and Curtis Maloley,[3] *Podagogy* by Austin Davis and Laura Milligan,[4] *Popular Podagogy* by the Faculty of Education at Queen's University,[5] and *Tes Podagogy* by the writers and editors of the *Times Educational Supplement.*[6] While none of these podcasters explain the term, it is evident that they are using this portmanteau word to signal that their medium is a podcast and their subject is Education research and practice. So, in invoking this term, they are not necessarily thinking about incorporating podcasts into teaching. Neil Verma's employment of the term is closer to the way in which I am using it because he deploys it to discuss the assimilation of podcasts in classroom teaching. He makes a further distinction between 'Podagogy 1.0', which is when existing podcasts or bespoke podcast episodes recorded by the instructor are

---

[2] Although podcasts do come in different formats, this Element is concerned with podcasts that provide commentary on Shakespeare through conversations, lectures, or interviews. This focus reflects the most common formats adopted by Shakespeare podcasters.

[3] www.ryerson.ca/centre-for-excellence-in-learning-and-teaching/teaching-resources/Podagogies/.

[4] https://soundcloud.com/podagogy-696048322.

[5] https://podcast.cfrc.ca/category/podagogy/.

[6] https://uk-podcasts.co.uk/podcast/tes-podagogy.

introduced and discussed in seminars to supplement lectures or reading material, and 'Podagogy 2.0', which 'emphasizes the integration of podcast creation on the part of students' (Verma, 2021: 142). Thus, in Podagogy 2.0, students 'learn "by" podcasting rather than "through" the podcasts of others' (142). I am taking advantage of the rising currency of and Verma's theorization of this term while also extending its purview and its application in feminist teaching. Feminist pedagogy, as I am defining it, involves thinking about and practicing ways in which podcasts usher feminist ways of teaching and learning. So, feminist podagogy includes using podcasts as repositories of information that is useful in feminist teaching in the sense of Podagogy 1.0, and it encourages students to create their own feminist podcasts along the lines of Podagogy 2.0. But it also entails putting more pressure on affordances of podcasts such as amplification, community building, or archiving that align with feminist methodologies in order to facilitate a gender-inclusive mode of teaching and foster feminist conversations.

Feminist approaches such as these are necessary for Shakespeare Studies because women have not been well served by Shakespeare higher education. One of the spaces in which this becomes visible in academia is the arena of conferences and public talks. For instance, in 2016, at the World Shakespeare Congress (WSC), which is perhaps 'one of the largest gatherings of Shakespeareans and early modernists on the planet' (Williams, 2016), this marginalization touched a nerve with many women delegates. Nora Williams (2016) reports how 'out of seven *advertised* plenary speakers ... there were two women and two people of colour – Ayanna Thompson, as a black woman, counts for one in each category, and she wasn't even speaking on her own'. This statistic was felt keenly by Williams, and she wondered 'to what extent are we complicit in perpetuating ... all-male, all-white panels, unbalanced plenary line-ups, and the comfortable notion that "working on it" is enough by our mere attendance? ... What but our continued, insistent presence can change the demographics of the decision makers?'. She was not the only one. Several others felt let down and took to the social media platform, Twitter, to air their dissatisfaction. One of the accounts which adopts the persona of William Shakespeare – that is, it imagines how Shakespeare might have written/tweeted were he on Twitter – tweeted satirically that 'when we hadn't any women on the stage, we'd at least dress up a few of the boys and fake it. #WSCongress16'.[7]

Furthermore, women whose identities intersect with other marginalized groups find themselves even more disadvantaged in Shakespeare higher education owing to a host of systemic factors. Wendy Lennon, founder of the 'Shakespeare, Race & Pedagogy' initiative and online event (2021), is a schoolteacher as well as a doctoral student in the United Kingdom (UK), and she writes about her 'anger and sadness at being silenced' (Lennon, 2021: 7) as a woman of colour from a working-class background. She explains that 'out of [her] supervisor's four students', she was the only one 'not to receive funding' for her research and reports that it was only in 2019 when she was first 'taught by a woman of colour' (Lennon, 2021: 7, 6). She recounts,

> the reason I wanted to create my event is because I didn't feel that there was a space for me and so I had to create my own. Even though I had made attempts to be involved, my voice wasn't allowed or welcomed. But, I feel that this work is so important. I know that it's beneficial for everybody and so I felt that I needed to do this and not just for me.[8]

Similarly, Farah Karim-Cooper, Co-director of Education at Shakespeare's Globe confides, 'growing up in the Shakespeare industry as an undergraduate, grad student, I didn't feel powerful as a female and perhaps a woman of colour as well. That feeling stays with you for quite some time and you get imposter syndrome, and you think "I don't belong in this field"' (Karim-Cooper, 2020). To these voices, I will add my own. Although I was lucky to be taught Shakespeare by a woman of colour as an undergraduate student,[9] I remember how much of a stranger I felt at Shakespeare conferences as a doctoral student and decided to avoid these events, even though these were deemed significant both to find a foothold in the field and to keep abreast of current research. As

---

[7]　See tweet: https://twitter.com/Shakespeare/status/761535087494230018.

[8]　Personal Communication, Informal Interview, January 2022.

[9]　I will forever be indebted to my lecturer Amina Alyal who taught me how to engage with Shakespeare.

further examples in Section 1 demonstrate, this was because, like the 2016 WSC, the keynote speakers were overwhelmingly men despite the number of female academics in 'English Language & Literature' area in the UK outweighing the number of male academics according to the data collected by the Higher Education Statistics Agency (HESA) for the period from 2014/15 to 2019/20 (HESA, 2021). So, the reverse statistic in conference keynotes signalled to me that voices such as mine were not worthy of an audience of Shakespeare experts.

Considering that Shakespeare carries immense cultural capital and is a prominent presence in the curriculum for English, Drama, and Liberal Arts degrees, the fact that women students and educators are made to feel outsiders in this field is worth pausing over. This situation is especially troubling since there is a long history of critical interventions in the field from the perspectives of Feminist Shakespeares, Queer Studies, Global Shakespeares, Postcolonial Studies, Early-modern Critical Race Studies, and Disability Studies, accompanied by struggles for diversity in casting and creating in Shakespeare cultural industries through which marginalized communities have both claimed a stake in the ownership of Shakespeare and demonstrated the value of interrogating his texts in relation to gender, race, sexuality, culture, and disability. However, due to structural and systemic inequalities, it takes more than the existence of scholarship or radical performances to produce a cultural shift. Speaking at the 'Shakespeare, Race & Pedagogy' event, Nandini Das points out that for her 'one of the most positive things that has emerged over the last couple of years' in academia is the

> recognition of absolute bedrock scholarship [in relation to Shakespeare and Race] that had already happened, in some cases, a couple of decades before this. Foundational work by people like Kim Hall, by Imtiaz Habib, by Jyotsna Singh, those are beginning to be examined and celebrated in a way that they hadn't perhaps been done in the wider academic network or academic landscape.
>
> (Das & Price, 2021)

Although Das is hopeful, her statement indicates that there is a gap of time before critical fields and scholarship that challenge race and gender hegemonies make their way into the mainstream critical trends, curricula, and teaching practice. It is telling that 2 out of the 3 scholars identified by Das are women of colour as it can take decades before research by women of colour is given acknowledgement and they get invited as keynote speakers or even given their due as experts in our classrooms. Another reason why developments in scholarship or performance do not automatically impact pedagogy either in practice or theory is that

> [d]espite formal education being the most common way in which the population encounters his work, and hence formative of attitudes towards it, education has been historically under-examined in scholarly Shakespearean publications and at international conferences. This is especially conspicuous in comparison to the volume of titles and seminars on performance history, literary criticism and the textual study of Shakespeare.
>
> (Olive, 2015: 4)

Perhaps this is why even monumental shifts in scholarship are often not examined in relation to pedagogy. For example, a Shakespeare academic notes how '[a]s a student of literature in the early 2000s, I did not encounter books such as [Kim F. Hall's] *Things of Darkness* or Ania Loomba's *Gender, Race, Renaissance Drama*' (Refskou, 2021) even though these monographs were first published in 1995 and 1987 respectively. As Kimberly Anne Coles, Hall, and Ayanna Thompson remind us, '[r]ecognition matters. In both our classrooms and in our research, it is important to remember John Guillory's maxim – the syllabus is the canon' (n.d.). So, this time lag and reluctance in recognition are, in turn, responsible for feelings of disempowerment that scores of women, including scholars such as Williams, Lennon, Karim-Cooper, Refskou, or I, have felt as students and educators in the field of Shakespeare Studies.

However, we are beginning to see a change and the interest generated by the 'Shakespeare, Race & Pedagogy' online event, which attracted 619 online attendees and over 500 views of the recorded sessions, exemplifies the increased focus on linking cutting-edge research with pedagogy. Sometimes this impetus has come from educators, although often 'our students are demanding it. They want these conversations to happen' (Karim-Cooper, 2020). But as we adopt digital technologies and Web 2.0 (or the participatory web) resources in our teaching, do we facilitate or hinder these advances? This is a question that has not received due attention from either Feminist Shakespeares or Shakespeare Digital Humanities (DH). The otherwise comprehensive and invaluable second edition of *A Feminist Companion to Shakespeare* (Callaghan, 2016) does not include a chapter on the interaction between digital tools and feminist theory, practice, or teaching. Digital Humanities in general has also been slow to take stock of pedagogy in its discussions. As Brett D. Hirsch (2012) argued, pedagogy is often an 'afterthought' or 'tacked-on' (5) in critical discussions of digital humanities. In *Digital Humanities Pedagogy*, he urges that 'we owe it to ourselves (and indeed to our students) to pay more than lip service to pedagogy in our field' (Hirsch, 2012: 6). Since Hirsch's call to action, several books and articles on digital tools have explicitly addressed pedagogical questions in Shakespeare Studies. Christie Carson and Peter Kirwan's edited collection *Shakespeare and the Digital World* (2014) and Stephen O Neill's *Shakespeare and YouTube* (2014) both carve out space for discussing digital Shakespeare pedagogy. The recently published *Shakespeare and Digital Pedagogy* (2022), edited by Diana E. Henderson and Kyle Sebastian Vitale, is entirely devoted to pedagogy, as the title suggests, and its contributors explore intersections between digital resources and the way in which these can be used to discuss gender, race, identity, culture, and performance, thereby strengthening that important connectivity between diverse Shakespeare scholarship and digital pedagogy. *Podcasts and Feminist Shakespeare Pedagogy* inserts podcasts into this conversation. While scholars in the Henderson and Vitale collection and elsewhere devote entire chapters or monographs to digital technologies such as blogs (Kirwan, 2014a), YouTube (O'Neill, 2014), Wikipedia (Moberly, 2018), databases (Ng-Gagneux, 2022; Rogers, 2022), virtual learning environments (Sullivan, 2014), and virtual reality (Wittek & McInnis, 2021) in Shakespeare teaching, the use of podcasts has not been discussed at length despite (or perhaps because of?) its attractiveness to women scholars and creatives.[10] In this

---

[10] Cyrus Mulready is the only contributor to include more than a brief reference to podcasting in Shakespeare teaching within these recent publications. He mentions that three of his students 'recorded a rich discussion about gender power

Element, I examine how digital humanities, Shakespeare, and feminist conversations intersect in twenty-first-century teaching through a detailed discussion of feminist podagogy or using podcasts as cyberfeminist educational tools in Shakespeare Studies.

One of the reasons for my optimism regarding podcasts is that the very technology that enabled it was born out of resistance. As Stommel (2014) reminds us, 'we are better users of technology when we are thinking critically about the nature and effects of that technology'. The origin story of podcasting indicates that the 'nature' of this technology might be amenable to feminist purposes. In 2001, Christopher Lydon and Mary McGarth were working on a radio show, 'The Connection' for WBUR, a station owned by Boston University. When they insisted on an ownership stake in the programme that they were making, Lydon and McGarth were suspended on grounds of insubordination. At the very time that they were looking for an alternative distribution outlet, Dave Winer, a blogger, had become successful at transporting sound files through RSS – the syndication technology that enables users to subscribe to a newsletter, blog, or a podcast and be notified when it is published. Winer, Lydon, and McGarth decided to collaborate and the latter's audio programme was shared through RSS feeds, giving birth to the podcasting technology in June 2003. So, podcasting was born out of resistance to ownership by a mainstream radio station.[11] Lydon asserts that 'podcasting is different to radio – institutionally as well as functionally' (quoted in Frizzell, 2016). He elaborates that it 'was born out of the despair around the Iraq War. It was a political response to a giant breakdown in the American conversation, in the world conversation. I went to New York to

and politics, following [their] study of *Twelfth Night*' in the form of a podcast episode. It is interesting that his students chose podcast as a medium for their discussion of gender power and politics as part his Digital Scribes assignment even though they had the choice to respond via 'a video, a multimedia webpage, a podcast, a collection of memes, an alternative lesson plan, a series of tweets, or other social media expressions' (Mulready, 2022: 19, 14). However, Mulready does not remark on the link or discuss podcasts any further.

[11] This account of podcasting's origin story is largely based on Sterne, Morris, Baker, & Freire (2008).

demonstrate and *The New York Times* didn't even cover it. Podcasting was about people speaking up in a time of traditional media oblivion' (quoted in Frizzell, 2016). Therefore, opposition to traditional forms of power and media is encoded in podcasting's DNA, making it a tool suited to feminist use.

Another reason to celebrate podcasting is that women are tuning in – at least in the United States of America (US) and UK. A special study on women podcast listeners in the US (Edison Research & Triton Digital, 2019) showed that the gap between men and women podcast listeners was rapidly closing in 2019. In a bid to dive deeper into podcast listener trends, when they surveyed 'rookie' (those who started listening in the last six months) and 'veteran' (those who started listening three or more years ago) monthly podcast listeners, they discovered that although the number of men who are veteran listeners is higher, the majority of rookies are women – a further testament to women's increasing adoption of the medium. Moreover, it was revealed that women, on average, listen to more podcasts per week and spend significantly longer time with podcasts compared to men. The 2020 study (Edison Research & Triton Digital, 2020) was more promising because the gender gap in monthly podcast listeners closed completely. The statistics are less impressive in the UK, with the 2020 Spring MIDAS (Measurement of Internet Delivered Audio Services) report (RAJAR – Radio Joint Audience Research, 2020) revealing that 46% of podcast listeners are women as compared to 54% men, but this data, too, is reflective of the US trend because this is an appreciable growth from the figures in the 2018 report (RAJAR, 2018) where women were only 37% of the listening population in the UK. Cumulatively, these figures are good news because there is a high chance that teachers will find women engaged and interested in this digital technology.

However, the sense of optimism at the heart of this Element is not jejune. The early cyberfeminists were enthused by the 'subversive potential of human/ machine cyborgs, identity tourism, and disembodiment' (Daniels, 2009: 101) that could be offered in cyberspace, but the critiques of these cyberfeminisms as well as the everyday experience of women using digital technologies have made it evident that offline oppressions of race and gender are persistently present online. This should be an important consideration for digital Shakespeare pedagogy. According to Claire Battershill and Shawna Ross (2017),

> when we think about using new technologies in the classroom,
> the hardest part is getting started. This is not because of a lack
> of available tools and methods, but rather a surfeit: when there
> are so many possibilities for activities, platforms and resources,
> it can be tremendously difficult to separate the useful from the
> useless and the time-saving from the time-consuming.
>
> (1)

It seems that Shakespeare educators have overcome the hardest part and employ a dizzying range of digital technologies in their teaching. Twitter, for instance, is a popular tool amongst academics because it functions 'as an asynchronous conference that never ends and takes all comers' (Ross quoted in Battershill & Ross, 2017: 185), and by using it in tandem with their seminars and courses, educators can include students in this conference. However, it is alarming when we juxtapose these educational possibilities with statements made by Twitter CEOs through the years:

> We suck at dealing with abuse and trolls on the platform and
> we've sucked at it for years . . . We lose core user after core user
> by not addressing simple trolling issues that they face every day.
> I'm frankly ashamed of how poorly we've dealt with this issue
> during my tenure as CEO. It's absurd. There's no excuse for it.
> (Dick Costolo, former Twitter CEO, quoted in Tiku &
> Newton, 2015)

> We see voices being silenced on Twitter every day. We've
> been working to counteract this for the past 2 years . . . We
> prioritized this in 2016. We updated our policies and increased
> the size of our teams. It wasn't enough.
> (Jack Dorsey, current Twitter CEO, 2017)[12]

> We love instant, public, global messaging and conversation. It's
> what Twitter is and it's why we're here. But we didn't fully

---

[12]　See his tweets: https://twitter.com/jack/status/919028949434241024.

predict or understand the real-world negative consequences. We acknowledge that now, and are determined to find holistic and fair solutions.

(Jack Dorsey, current Twitter CEO, 2018)[13]

While Costolo and Dorsey do not admit the gendered or racial nature of this abuse or trolling, it is clear that women are one of its targets. According to Amnesty International's online poll (2017), which tracked women's experiences of abuse and harassment on social media platforms across eight countries, including the US and UK, Twitter emerged as the top social media platform for such abuse. Moreover, '[w]omen of colour, in particular, emphasized to Amnesty International that in addition to Twitter manifesting existing patriarchal structures in society, ideologies of white supremacy are also permeating into the platform' (Amnesty International, 2017).

Twitter is not the only offender. YouTube is another resource that is used widely in Shakespeare teaching. In his book-length study on the connection between this video-creating and sharing platform and Shakespeare, O'Neill (2014) argues that YouTube is 'a valuable learning resource' for Shakespeare because it functions both as an archive that 'provides learners with access to a wealth of Shakespeare content' and as a tool through which 'learners can be encouraged to adopt a participatory role in (re)making Shakespeare', but he cautions that there is a 'need for a critical, rather than celebratory, attitude to YouTube as a Shakespeare learning resource' because this 'new platform can return old blind spots and stereotypes about Shakespeare texts' (191, 207, 191). However, it is not only a multiplication of problematic interpretations with regards to gender, race, and sexuality in Shakespeare that we need to fear. Replicating and refining an earlier study, Nicola Döring and M. Rohangis Mohseni (2019) too reached the conclusion that 'male dominance and sexism are visible problems on YouTube' (10). Women are 'clearly underrepresented in the top 100 YouTube channels of nine different countries' but they showed that this bias on YouTube is, surprisingly, greater 'than in traditional media' (10). They further concluded that 'female YouTubers seem to be prone to receiving more negative and hostile video comments',

---

[13] See his tweets: https://twitter.com/jack/status/969234278167949313.

especially if 'they do not conform to gender role expectations' (10). Therefore, as we ask learners to engage with YouTube, we need to be equipping them to ask questions about the nature of this archive and to register the challenges of their participation.

If we look at the collaborative information sharing platform, Wikipedia, another resource that students use whether or not educators approve of it, the 'gender gap' in its contributors and the harassment that women editors face on the site are documented and supported with evidence in Wikipedia's own entry, 'Gender bias on Wikipedia'.[14] David C. Moberly (2018: 88, 103) has demonstrated that this bias affects the Wikipedia entry on Shakespeare. He rightly contends that 'for those scholars who are serious about public engagement and public education regarding Shakespeare', we cannot afford to ignore a 'male centric Shakespeare that Wikipedia has created'. He suggests that 'a small, committed network of Shakespeare scholars could turn things around, diversify and broaden the content' (Moberly, 2018: 104) of the Shakespeare page. A 'small' network might be able to turn things around as far as the Wikipedia Shakespeare entry is concerned, but it is important to acknowledge the sheer scale of racism and sexism that can be encountered while using these online resources such as Wikipedia, YouTube, and Twitter.

According to Amnesty International's poll (2017) mentioned earlier, nearly a quarter of the women surveyed across the eight countries said that they had experienced online abuse or harassment at least once, including those in UK and the US. If we look at the findings of another 2020 survey (Glitch & The End Violence Against Women Coalition, 2020) that examined online behaviours during the COVID-19 pandemic, the figures are similarly distressing. The survey was limited to women and non-binary individuals and it found that

- 46% of respondents reported experiencing online abuse since the beginning of COVID-19. This figure increased to 50% for Black and minoritized women and nonbinary people.
- Of the respondents who had experienced online abuse in the 12 months preceding the survey, 29% reported it being worse during COVID-19.

[14] https://en.wikipedia.org/wiki/Gender_bias_on_Wikipedia.

▪ Gender was the most often cited reason for online abuse. 48% of respondents reported suffering from gender-based abuse.

(Glitch & The End Violence Against Women Coalition, 2020: 7, 8)

It is obvious that COVID-19 restrictions and the related move to spending increased amounts of time online has only intensified the problems and has led to a corresponding 'epidemic of online abuse' (Glitch & The End Violence Against Women Coalition, 2020) against women, as the subtitle of the report suggests. It has further reinforced the barriers for women navigating digital technologies.

In her powerful book, *Living a Feminist Life*, Sara Ahmed (2017) draws our attention to the way in which 'walls often come up when we are doing diversity work'. She describes such brick walls as 'hardenings of histories into barriers in the present'. However, these walls are 'only obstacles for some bodies' (135, 136). Women, especially women belonging to marginalized racial groups, are these 'some bodies' who are stopped by these institutional brick walls. I contend that beyond these institutional walls, in the World Wide Web, women are met with firewalls. In technical terms, a firewall is a 'network security device that monitors incoming and outgoing network traffic and permits or blocks data packets based on a set of security rules' (Forcepoint, n.d.). So, a firewall is a highly selective wall that is not experienced as a barrier or a wall for some agents while it blocks others. Whether an agent is allowed or not depends on 'security rules' that are 'pre-established' and 'filter traffic coming from unsecured or suspicious sources to prevent attacks' (Forcepoint, n.d.). We can think of cyberspace as full of firewalls for women. Not firewalls that protect them but firewalls that instead block them because they did not play by 'pre-established rules' or were deemed suspicious. The firewalls experienced by women online are very real in the way that Ahmed (2017) explains when she talks about the reality of institutional brick walls: 'it is not that there really is a wall; it is not an actual wall. This is right. The wall is a wall that might as well be there, because the effects of what is there are just like the effects of a wall' (137–8). Similarly, there is no actual firewall against women in cyberspace, but it is also more than a mere metaphor because the effects produced are the same as if there actually were such a firewall. If we look at more data from the Amnesty International (2017) report, this effect becomes clear. Of the women polled who experienced online abuse or harassment, between 63% and 83% women in the eight countries polled made some changes to the way they used social media platforms, with the figures for the US and UK being 81% and 78%, respectively. These figures were similar to the data in the Glitch & The End Violence Against Women Coalition (2020) report in which '77% of respondents testified modifying their behaviour online as a result of the abuse, and 72% confessed to feeling differently about using technology and social media' (8). These changes might include self-censoring, fundamentally changing the way in which they use these platforms, limiting their interactions or leaving these platforms completely (Amnesty International, 2017). So, there might not be an obvious firewall against women, but the firewall effect of rejecting and blocking is certainly evident, and the 'pre-established' settings have sexism coded into them. This code is the result of a 'hardening of histories' of abuse both offline and online. In other words, prejudices from the offline world are carried over, sometimes more aggressively, to online environments. The abuse is not limited to social media but extends to the entirety of the web where we might obtain, publicize, or home our digital Shakespeare resources. As Tim Berners-Lee, the inventor of the World Wide Web, put it, the Internet 'is not working for women and girls' (quoted in Sample, 2020). So, when we look to the web to teach Shakespeare, we cannot afford to overlook the culture of hostility and silencing of women that we are asking our students to inhabit. However, as education technology writer Audrey Watters (2014) cautions, the 'answer can't simply be "don't blog on the open Web". Or "keep everything inside the 'safety' of the walled garden, the learning management system"'. Moodle, Blackboard, and Turnitin are the most frequently used software programs in education technology and the current CEOs of all three of these companies are White and male. Although it is difficult to generalize effects from this fact alone, we do need to probe the gender and ethnic make-up of software designers of these systems further and understand how their 'privileges, ideologies, expectations, values get hard-coded into ed-tech [educational technology]' (Watters, 2014). Such work falls beyond the purview of this Element, but it is sorely needed. In her groundbreaking study, *Race*

After Technology, Ruha Benjamin (2019) exposed how, from everyday apps to complex algorithms, technology itself is encoded as racist so it is pertinent to pay attention to how education technology, too, can create gender- and race-exclusionary learning environments.

Even in the virtual world, then, there is nothing new under the sun. However, if uncritical enthusiasm about digital technologies is naïve, then a narrative that only registers gender oppression also overshadows the way in which cyberfeminists have used and are using digital technologies for innovation, organization, resistance, and subversion of repressive race and gender hierarchies. To invoke the visionary Black science fiction writer, Olivia Butler, more explicitly, 'There is nothing new / Under the sun / But there are new suns'. Benjamin (2017) glosses these words to reinforce that although Butler's words 'acknowledge the "nothing new" status quo that everywhere surrounds us' they also invoke 'a restless resistance to submitting to that quo' (103). Even if we cast the most cursory glance at such restless resistance in the cybersphere, we can find the chatbot 'Ladymouth' (Ciston, 2019) that is coded to respond to online misogyny with quotations from feminist theorists, or we will discover a host of listservs set up by and catering to the communities of women from the South Asian diaspora (Gajjala, 2003), or we can listen to the *Brown Girls Do It Too* podcast which provides candid insights into personal experiences of sex and relationships of Brown girls,[15] or we could participate in '#HashtagActivism' such as #SayHerName, #MeToo, #GirlsLikeUs which as Sarah J. Jackson, Moya Bailey, and Brooke Foucault Welles (2020) have explained are used by marginalized groups to galvanize networks of dissent and challenge mainstream narratives. In the context of Shakespeare Studies, we can register Twitter groups formed around #ShakeRace set up by activist educators in the field. Although their organizers and users concede that the online groups 'cannot substitute for the depth of in-person dialogue, such mechanisms can be used for professional training until we have more on-site faculty supervision of this work' (Coles, Hall, & Thompson, n.d.). #ShakeRace is now used by scholars to find mentorship, resources, community, and share the latest developments and debates in the field of Shakespeare and Critical Race Studies. Another online

---

[15] www.bbc.co.uk/programmes/p08k5cp0.

example of activist scholarship is the TIDE project (Travel, Transculturality and Identity in England, 1550–1700) led by Das as it provides extensive history and resources on migration and identity through its website.[16] Further examples include the already mentioned 'Shakespeare, Race & Pedagogy' enterprise in which technology played a huge role in facilitating the conversation. As Lennon told me, 'all [she] had was frustration, so much sadness, an internet connection, and a laptop'.[17] Finally, I would add the *Women & Shakespeare* podcast to the list as it uses the digital technology of podcasts to amplify women's voices in the field. That all these initiatives are led and nurtured by women of colour is testament to the ways in which digital technologies can be used and are being used for intersectional feminist work.

In the face of both oppressions and liberations, we need a critical attitude towards digital tools that we employ and digital spaces that we occupy in Shakespeare pedagogy. This is a matter of pressing concern as more and more digital methodologies and resources form part of our teaching. As critical digital pedagogy theorists and practitioners have been warning us, 'tools are made by people, and most (or even all) educational technologies have pedagogies hard-coded into them in advance. This is why it is so essential that we consider them carefully and critically . . . some tools are decidedly less innocuous than others. And some tools can never be hacked to good use' (Friend, 2016). One of the reasons why digital resources might escape scrutiny in teaching is that 'the speed at which new technologies are adopted does not always leave time for *pedagogic* reflection on how and why they are being used' (Kirwan, 2014b: 58). If these were the circumstances when Kirwan pointed this out in 2014, then the scenario in the 2020s is even more challenging with educators having had to restructure their courses for online delivery within a matter of days in the COVID-19 pandemic. While academics were supplied with many online tools, resources, and how-to manuals, critical assessment and reflection were increasingly left out.

---

[16] www.tideproject.uk/.
[17] Personal Communication. Informal Interview. January 2022.

Even when critical appraisal of digital tools and resources is considered, it is peer review that is given utmost prominence. For instance, Battershill and Ross (2017) recommend that students and scholars using digital technologies should 'look for signs of institutional scholarship ... such resources may also come from grants, which is a positive sign because it means the project has undergone peer review' (29–30). This point crops up again when they write that 'positive reviews in academic journals obviously represent even more transparent and detailed peer evaluation' (30). However, marginalized scholars have demonstrated that peer review is not a guarantor of quality as much as a gatekeeping mechanism. In her chapter on the process of publishing in academia, Dale Spender corroborates Thomas Kuhn's assertion that 'those who have established reputations (and who are likely to be editors, reviewers, or advisors) often have a vested interest in preserving the authority of their work and can suppress fundamental novelties which challenge, or reflect unfavourably on their work' (Spender, 1981: 191). She argues that 'women are by no means the only "outsiders" but they are a significant group' (191) and may well suffer through the lack of transparency in the peer-reviewing process. Even in 2020, the academic journal *PMLA* rejected a cluster of essays on premodern Critical Race Studies which raised questions about deep systemic biases in the peer-reviewing process (ACMRS Arizona, 2020). In the case of digital humanities, insisting on peer review and institutional funding as the primary markers of quality becomes even more suspect given that

> [m]any scholars originally were drawn to the digital humanities because we felt like outcasts, because we had been marginalized within the academic community. We gathered together because our work collectively disrupted the hegemony and insularity of the 'traditional' humanities. Our work was collaborative, took risks, flattened hierarchies, shared resources, and created new and risky paradigms for humanities work.
>
> (Kim & Stommel, 2018: 20)

In other words, the critical evaluation that these resources need to be subjected to is not peer review but an appraisal of these tools in relation to class, race, and gender. As Dorothy Kim (2018) suggests, '[d]igital methods classes must stop being just about tools. They must include a balance of discussing critical issues like race, gender, disability, multimodality, sexuality, etc.' (490).

This Element adopts the theory and framework of cyberfeminism to examine the use of podcasts in Shakespeare pedagogy – a concept and methodology that I am calling feminist podagogy. Therefore, feminist podagogy is attentive to 'the ways in which digital technologies both subvert and reinscribe gender, race, and other corporeal hierarchies in virtual space' as well as embracing the spirit of 'productive and ironic play of cyberfeminist activism and theory' (Richards, 2011: 6, 7). The sections that follow develop this methodology by demonstrating that the affordances of podcasts can be utilized for feminist Shakespeare pedagogy. Section 1 discusses the public voices of two Shakespeare characters – Ophelia in *Hamlet* and Paulina in *The Winter's Tale* – and then observes how the aural misogyny of Shakespeare's world finds a counterpart in the field of Shakespeare Studies which sidelines the voices of women scholars. It traces the effect that this sound of scholarship has on our students and contends that podcasts are helping and can help to break the cycle of reinscribing this bias by amplifying the voices of women scholars in the field. Section 2 argues that we can participate in intersectional cyberfeminist activism by using podcasts to record and archive actresses' insights into playing Shakespeare's characters. Concentrating on Jessica in *The Merchant of Venice* and Celia in *As You Like It*, it shows how access to such a resource would develop a counter-performance history which can encourage feminist readings of the plays in our seminars. Finally, Section 3 includes detailed 'podagogical' activities and assignments that can be employed to engage with feminism in Shakespeare Studies. Even as these sections urge a feminist diversifying of Shakespeare pedagogy, they are limited in scope because they concentrate on UK/US Higher Education settings and English-language Shakespeare podcasts owing to my experience, which is limited to UK/US Higher Education teaching. However, my hope is that this initial work can pave the way for creating more inclusive podcasting spaces and practicing feminist and anti-racist podagogy in other educational settings in Shakespeare Studies.

1 Amplify: The Public Voice of Women in Shakespeare and Podcasts

On 8 October 2020, a video clip was shared widely online; in cyber parlance, the clip 'went viral'. It stitched together those moments of the US vice-presidential debate in which Senator Kamala Harris repeatedly pointed out the obvious – 'Mr Vice President, I'm speaking, I'm speaking' – because her opponent, Mike Pence, was talking over her.[18] Perhaps it resonated with so many women generally and with women of colour specifically because they heard echoes of their own experiences in Harris' vocalization and Pence's attempt at dismissing her speech. Unfortunately, this moment has a robust history; in 'The Public Voice of Women', Mary Beard (2014) takes a long view of the 'culturally awkward relationship between the voice of women and the public sphere' (11) in the West. She quotes from one of the foundational cultural texts, *The Odyssey*, in which Telemachus, the son of Odysseus and Penelope, declares to his mother that 'speech will be the business of men, all men'. Significantly, Beard elaborates that the word Telemachus uses for speech is '*muthos*', which 'signals authoritative public speech (not the kind of chatting, prattling or gossip that anyone – women included, or specially women – could do)' (11) and, according to him, *muthos* will be the exclusive purview of men. Early twentieth-century broadcasting trends also reveal such vocal prejudice. For instance, the British Broadcasting Corporation (BBC) hired their first woman announcer, Giles Borrett, only in 1933 and terminated her contract after a mere three months despite her garnering praise for her performance because listeners objected to a woman's voice in an announcer's role (McKay, 1988 reprinted in 2000: 22). The story was similar in the US where the National Broadcasting Company (NBC) appointed Elsie Janis as their first woman announcer in 1935 and 'listeners complained that a woman's voice was inappropriate', so her employer announced that she would 'read no more Press-Radio news bulletins' (*Newsweek* quoted in McKay, 1988 reprinted in 2000: 22). More generally, as summarized by Christine Mottram (2016: 53–9), numerous twenty-first-century studies also indicate that masculine voice qualities such as lower pitch, deeper

---

[18] Kamala Harris won the election to become the vice president of the US. The clip can be found here: https://youtu.be/tXFqTGBty1w.

oral and chest resonance, downward inflection at the end of the thought, clear tone achieved by breath support are perceived as having more authority. Although these vocal features can be found in women's voices, men are physiologically more likely to possess them, so 'it is still the case that when listeners hear a female voice, they don't hear a voice that connotes authority' (Beard, 2014: 14). This sonic marginalization is not only gendered but also racial. Building on the work of Jennifer Stoever and W.E.B. DuBois, David Sterling Brown (2021) explains that 'race gets in the way' of registering Black voices or voices of people of colour as authoritative because the dominant White listening practices set the tone for who is perceived as worth hearing and paying attention to. It is, therefore, no surprise that women of colour are the most overlooked public speakers.

I began by juxtaposing one moment belonging to the past of classical antiquity and another that captured the cultural zeitgeist in 2020, or one instance from literature and another from a live event, because Shakespeare Studies in the West reflects these patterns: on the one hand, Shakespeare's plays depict numerous scenes in which women struggle to be heard in public because society demands (or at least expects) their silence and, on the other hand, the voices of women scholars are marginalized in scholarly discourse even today. Taken together, Shakespearean cultures – the fictional societies that Shakespeare creates as well as the scholarly community within which his work is studied – engender an environment in which women are not fully included as participants in public conversation. This becomes doubly disempowering for women students of Shakespeare who thus encounter two worlds which sideline women's public speech. Such a culture also neglects to teach men students to hear authority in a woman's voice.

This section contends that podcasts, due to their emphasis on public voice, can participate in tackling this issue and offer students a chance to experience a scholarly discourse that does not end up reifying the gendered aural marginalization contained within (and often critiqued by) Shakespeare's plays. First, it provides detailed case studies of two very different women characters in Shakespeare: Ophelia, a young unmarried girl in *Hamlet*, and Paulina, a mature married woman in *The Winter's Tale*.[19] It examines the way in which their

---

[19] Unless otherwise noted, all in-text citations of *Hamlet* are from W. Shakespeare, *Hamlet*, A. Thompson and N. Taylor, eds. London: Bloomsbury, 2006a.

public voices are policed and emphasizes how women resist aural control in Shakespeare's worlds. Next, it studies the resonance of these silencing cultures in the milieu of Shakespeare Studies today and considers its impact on our students. Finally, it concentrates on how podcasts can function as a resistance technology and amplify women's voices in the field. By situating podcasts in the context of both the diminishing of women's voices and women's opposition to such silencing in Shakespeare's texts and our academic soundscape, this section carves out an important role for feminist podagogy and demonstrates how podcasts can contribute towards a cyberfeminist Shakespeare pedagogy.

1.1 Ophelia: 'Pray you mark'

In the second scene of the first act of *Hamlet*, the audience meets the Danish court. According to the 1623 First Folio (F1) text of the play, this includes '*Claudius, King of Denmark, Gertrude the Queen, Hamlet, Polonius, Laertes and his sister Ophelia, Lords Attendant*' (1.2.SD). Although she is not included in the stage directions of either the First Quarto (Q1) or the Second Quarto (Q2), in F1, Ophelia is present in the first entry of the court party, a textual variant which has proved attractive to stage and screen directors because it both offers a chance to see Gertrude and Ophelia 'among a multitude of men' who are busy conducting state affairs and affords an opportunity to 'see this young woman on stage in company with Hamlet' (Rosenberg, 1992: 36–7), her love interest. However, Ophelia is the only named character in this list of entrants who has no lines in this scene. Whether she manages to communicate non-verbally or not, it is evident that it is rare for Ophelia to speak in company. In a more domestic conversation, Ophelia teases her brother that he should not act like 'ungracious pastors' who show others the 'steep and thorny way to heaven' while they themselves thread the 'primrose path of dalliance' (1.3.98–99) when he

All in-text citations of the First Folio (F1) and the First Quarto (Q1) texts of the play are from W. Shakespeare, *Hamlet: The Texts of 1603 and 1623*, A. Thompson and N. Taylor, eds. London: Bloomsbury, 2006b. All in-text citations of *The Winter's Tale* are from W. Shakespeare, *The Winter's Tale*, S. Snyder and D. T. Curren-Aquino, eds. New York: Cambridge University Press, 2007.

dispenses advice on her love life. She then reasons with her father Polonius that Hamlet has 'made many tenders / Of his affection' (1.3.98–99) towards her, 'hath importuned [her] with love / In honourable fashion' (1.3.109–10), and has accompanied his speech with 'almost all holy vows of heaven' (1.3.113) when he is objecting to their courtship. These utterances demonstrate that Ophelia can be playful or engage in an argument. So, she is quiet at court not because she is inarticulate but because it seems that this is what is expected of her in Shakespeare's Denmark.

Here, Shakespeare's Danish court mirrors Early-modern English society which similarly restricted women's public speech. Even humanist scholars, who supported women's education, demurred over the question of women speaking publicly. In his influential treatise, *The Instruction of a Christen Woman*, Juan Luis Vives, tutor to Mary Tudor, at first seems to support the idea of women's public speaking when he praises eloquent women from classical antiquity. He cites the example of Hortensia, 'the daughter of Hortensius the orator', who 'did so resemble her father's eloquence, that she made an oration unto the judges of the city for the women, which oration the successors of that time did read, not only as a laud and praise of women's eloquence, but also to learn the cunning of it, as well as of Cicero or Demosthenes orations' (C3r).[20] However, when he starts to design a syllabus for women, he writes that 'as for eloquence I have no great care, nor a woman needeth it not' (C4v). There is more to Vives' omission than simply the argument that women did not need such training because they could not practice law or hold political appointments that would require public speaking. Rather, he suggests that such public speaking would be unseemly in a woman:

> It neither becometh a woman to rule a school, nor to live among men, or speak abroad, and shake off her demureness and honesty, either all together or else a great part: which if she be good, it were better to be at home within and unknown

---

[20] While quoting from texts printed in the Early modern period, I have modernized the spelling and capitalization, except for the book titles, but I have retained italics. References to Vives' work are from its English translation by Richard Hyrde (*c.* 1528).

to other folks. And in company to hold her tongue demurely.
And let few see her, and none at all hear her

(D1r).

Apparently, being heard is to be more strictly controlled than being seen. Similarly, Richard Brathwait, in his complete behavioural guide for the English gentlewomen, writes that it is advisable for a young woman 'to tip her tongue with silence' (1631: N1r). It is unsurprising, therefore, that 'feminist historians have concluded that women's education in the period served primarily to close off the possibility of achieving a public voice' (Richards & Thorne, 2007: 5).

A public voice is something that Ophelia does not exercise in her next court scene, 2.2, where she is, once more, a silent presence. Before this scene, Polonius has chastised his daughter and has commanded her that she is not to 'give words or talk with the Lord Hamlet' (1.4.133), but when he discovers that Hamlet has visited his daughter in a disturbed state after she obeyed Polonius' injunction, he decides to confer with Claudius and Gertrude and takes Ophelia with him. Once there, he discusses the Hamlet and Ophelia relationship with the king and queen, reads out a letter that Hamlet has written to Ophelia, gives them details of Hamlet's 'solicitings' (2.2.123), and engineers a meeting between his daughter and Hamlet which he intends to spy upon with Claudius from 'behind an arras' (2.2.160). All this time, Ophelia is in attendance but does not utter a word. Some modern editors of the play are unsure of her inclusion in the scene even though all three textual variants of the play indicate her presence.[21] In Q1, there is an explicit stage direction that she is to enter with her father; in Q2, Polonius indicates twice that Ophelia is to accompany him when he says 'Come, go we to the King' (2.1.114) followed by the command, 'Come' (2.1.117); similarly, in F1, he asks Ophelia to 'Go

---

[21] Cedric Watts, for instance, writes in the editorial note that Polonius 'enters without Ophelia even though at 2.1.114 he had said to her "Come, go we to the King". That Shakespeare changed his mind is less surprising than that (according to early printed texts) nobody removed the inconsistency' (2002: 157). Also, Robert Hapgood believes that 'only in Q1, however, does she actually go with him to the King at this point' (1999: 150).

with me' (2.1.99) and follows it with 'Come, go we to the King' (2.1.115). So, the editorial confusion is caused by the fact that Ophelia does not speak at all and neither is she overtly addressed in this scene. An actress playing Ophelia would have to decide how uncomfortable she is when her father is reading out Hamlet's private letter to her, or how complicit she is with Polonius' plan to use her to spy on Hamlet. Whatever interpretation she chooses, she has been given no words or voice. This silence, however, is hardly surprising if seen in the context of 3.1 when Hamlet and Ophelia have a disturbing clash which is observed by Claudius and Polonius. Emerging from their hiding place, both ignore Ophelia completely as they continue their discussion of Hamlet's madness. When Ophelia perhaps tries to interpose, Polonius further shuts down her speech: 'How now, Ophelia? / You need not tell us what Lord Hamlet said – / We heard it all' (3.1.179). Glossing the performance possibilities of these lines in their edition of the play, Ann Thompson and Neil Taylor speculate that 'Polonius' speech can be made to express either kindness (he spares Ophelia the pain of having to recount her experience) or cruelty (he dismisses her and her pain without further thought)' (Shakespeare, 2006a: 294). Whether through kindness or cruelty, patronizing protectiveness or threat, deliberate dismissal, or casual ignoring, the result is the same: Ophelia's public speech is curbed in the first part of the play.

This dynamic changes in the latter part of the play. Alongside Ophelia's behaviour, her ability to speak at court alters too. For instance, in 3.2, or the play-within-the-play scene, she begins to rebuff Hamlet's insults. When Hamlet keeps explaining (mansplaining?) the action of the inset play, Ophelia taunts him, 'You are as good as a chorus, my lord' (3.2.238) and when he turns on her with a sexual barb, she critiques that he speaks 'still better and worse' (3.2.244). Although Hamlet tries to silence her by shaming her, the play begins to show us an Ophelia who is finding a public voice. This is also apparent later in the play when, even before Ophelia enters in 4.5, a messenger describes how Ophelia:

> Spurns enviously at straws, speaks things in doubt
> That carry but half sense. Her speech is nothing,
> Yet the unshaped use of it doth move
> The hearers to collection.

(4.5.6–9)

Howsoever 'unshaped' the use might be, her speech does not appear to be 'nothing' because, as the messenger himself reports, 'She speaks much of her father, says she hears / There's tricks i'th' world' (4.5.4–5) and this, he records, is affecting the hearers. Gertrude reverses her decision to give Ophelia an audience because Horatio in Q2 or Gertrude in F1 realizes the sociopolitical critique that Ophelia offers and fears that her words, spoken in public 'may strew / Dangerous conjectures in ill-breeding minds' (Q2: 4.5.14–15; F1: 4.1.14–15). However, this is also the instant in which Ophelia is branded as 'distract' (4.5.2). Mapping this link between mental disability, gender, and acquiring a space for public speaking, Tobin Siebers (2016) argues, there is 'reason in [Ophelia's] madness, and the reason is the sex-gender system'. What the court considers madness is the 'product of Ophelia's rebellion against everything supposedly known of her as a woman' (448, 449) which includes her combative stance towards gendered silencing. However, he asserts that Ophelia claims and embraces this disabled identity because it allows her to display 'non-normative' behaviour. Advancing a theory of complex embodiment of disability, he expounds that 'Ophelia discovers that to be a woman in a sexist society is to be disabled. But the knowledge of this disability requires the vehicle of another disability, in this case, madness, if it is to be communicated' (450). While scholars (including Siebers) have written about the way in which Ophelia claims 'public space through song and dance' or 'through feminine retelling of the stories' (Luiggi, 2016: 79) or through complex embodiment of mental disability, what is less noticed is that she asserts herself through spoken words too. It is interesting to note how commanding her vocabulary is and how often she is interrupted once she starts to speak.[22] The first interruption comes from Gertrude when she asks Ophelia 'what imports this song?' Marvin

---

[22] See Deanne Williams (2012) who argues that in the Q1 text of the play, Ofelia 'sings songs that are perfectly chosen to express her deep feelings' and when she performs with a lute as the stage directions in Q1 indicate, she 'is given time and space to perform, to express herself, and to be heard'. She also remarks how 'no one in Q1 has the temerity to interrupt Ofelia, whom we can imagine, in contemporary terms, as a folk singer, with a prepared play list and some remarks for the audience' (124, 127). It seems that the more Ophelia's words resemble public speech rather than the sanctioned performance of song, the more she is interrupted.

Rosenberg (1992) describes the way in which most Ophelias (including one in a Norwegian production of the play) have reacted and interpreted their next line, 'Say you? Nay, pray you, mark' (4.5.28):

> Ophelia will not bear interruption, has stamped her foot, shaken her head ... The Norway Gertrude tried to get away; Ophelia, like an Ancient Mariner, held her fast. What looks next like a question has been a retort: keep quiet!
>
> (779)

In this scene, therefore, Ophelia turns the tables and begins imposing the silence that was initially forced upon her by others. Gertrude tries to intervene a second time, 'Nay, but Ophelia-' (4.5.34) only for Ophelia to implore or command her, 'pray you mark' (4.5.35). When Gertrude stops interposing, Claudius tries to speak to her by asking, 'How do you, pretty lady?' (4.5.41) to which Ophelia replies, 'Well, god dild you. They say the owl was a baker's daughter. Lord, we know what we are but we know not we may be' (4.5.42–44). Ophelia's reply is cryptic but no more so than Hamlet's in 3.2 when Claudius asks him, 'how fares our cousin Hamlet?' (3.2.88), and Hamlet replies, 'Excellent, i'faith! Of the chameleon's dish – I eat the air promise-crammed' (3.2.89–90). Whether an actress decides that Ophelia is mad, or 'distract' with grief, or feigning madness, or, as Siebers points out, embracing madness because it allows her to express herself publicly in this sexist society, she has learnt to use speech in a way that thwarts inquiries. When Claudius tries to offer his own interpretation of Ophelia's song as 'conceit upon her father' (4.5.45), Ophelia stops him from doing so by saying, 'Pray, let's have no words of this' (4.5.46). Again, Rosenberg (1992) collates how different actresses have played this moment: 'she has put a finger to her lips, an innocent wronged; but she has also been fiery, demanding silence, scorning Claudius, screaming, threatening him, beating on his chest' (784). Her dialogue makes it clear that she is not to be disturbed but Claudius continues to do so by approaching her with, 'Pretty Ophelia-' (4.5.56). However, this time she is vehement and declares that 'Indeed, without an oath I'll make an end on't' (4.5.57). Although she does continue speaking, these scenes prove that women's public speech is a highly contested site. As Sandra Fischer puts it, it is 'not surprising that [Ophelia's] refrain in her madness is "Pray you mark"' (1990: 7). She has to keep reminding her audience that 'I'm speaking, I'm speaking'.

1.2 'O, peace, Paulina!'

Unlike Ophelia, who tries to speak truth to power in her final scenes, Paulina in *The Winter's Tale* dares to do so right from her first appearance at court. Like Ophelia, however, she is interrupted constantly. Paulina's first public utterances are in 2.3 in which she chastises Leontes, the King of Sicilia, for committing his innocent wife, Hermione, to prison due to his jealousy. At the entrance itself, she is stopped by an attendant Lord and she tries to reason that he should let her pass because he should fear for the Queen's life more than the 'tyrannous passion' (2.3.28) of Leontes. Paulina's husband, Antigonus, is the first one to tell her that 'That's enough!' (2.3.30). Next, Leontes enters and demands, 'What *noise* there, ho?' (2.3.39, emphasis mine). Editors Susan Snyder and Deborah T. Curren-Aquino (2007) note that Leontes' question is prompted by the fact that he is 'on another part of the stage, with his view of Paulina and the Lords blocked' so he has 'heard only commotion and not the actual altercation' (130). However, another performance possibility is that Leontes is deliberately undermining Paulina's words as inconsequential 'noise' rather than language even before she has the chance to speak to him. Paulina's next lines when she says, 'no noise, my lord, but needful conference' (2.3.40) give the impression that this is how she has interpreted Leontes' meaning.

Once Paulina is in the presence of Leontes, he tries another tactic to dismiss her words: he does not address her directly and instead speaks about her in the third person as 'that audacious lady' (2.3.42) or berates Antigonus, 'What? Canst not rule her?' (2.3.46). Antigonus also speaks *about* her instead of *to* her when he answers, 'La you now, you *hear*, / When she will take the rein, I let her run; / But she'll not stumble' (2.3.50–52, emphasis mine). Even as Antigonus draws attention to Paulina's speech, he continues to unhear her by addressing Leontes rather than Paulina. Despite this, Paulina continues to argue her case and starts to deliver and direct her speeches not only to Leontes and Antigonus but to the entire court of men when she begins, 'Behold, my lords' (2.3.97) and draws their attention to the infant, Perdita, she has been carrying; she argues that they can verify for themselves how much this baby girl whom Hermione has delivered resembles Leontes, leaving little doubt about her paternity. Leontes' mistreatment increases in intensity with Paulina's skill in oratory and he subjects her to a whole battery of verbal abuse: from 'A callat / Of boundless tongue' (2.3.90–91) to 'a mankind witch' (2.3.67) and 'a most intelligencing bawd' (2.3.68). While, at first glance, the last two accusations might appear unrelated to public speaking, scholars such as Kathleen Smith (2017) and Peter Stallybrass (1986: 123–42), amongst others, have shown how women speaking in public were associated with witches and carried the charge of wantonness in the early modern imaginary. Rather than her actions or behaviour, Leontes is fixated on Paulina's speech and remarks that Antigonus is 'worthy to be hanged' (2.3.108) because he 'wilt not stay her tongue' (2.3.109).

In Shakespeare's time, a woman like Paulina would have faced immediate physical threat because Early-modern England had torture devices that were designed for silencing women's public speech. One of the most frightening of these was the bridle – a contraption used to punish a 'scold'. Combing legal records for a definition of the term, Lynda Boose (1991) concludes that 'since this almost exclusively female category was defined by an exclusively male constabulary, and since the number of charges for verbal disruption brought against males are by comparison negligible, one can speculate that a "scold" was, in essence, any woman who verbally resisted or flouted authority publicly and stubbornly enough to challenge the underlying dictum of male rule' (189). Paulina, thus, qualifies for the term and risks the kind of punishment meted out to Dorothy Waugh – a historical figure who, in 1656, decided to 'speak against all deceit and ungodly practices' (D1r) in the Carlisle marketplace and challenged the Mayor and his officers. Her defiant act led the Mayor to punish her with a bridle which she describes as follows:

> [It] was a stone weight of Iron by the relation of their own generation, & three bars of iron to come over my face, and a peece of it was put in my mouth, which was so unreasonable big a thing for that place as cannot be well related,

which was locked to my head, and so I stood their time with my hands bound behind me with the stone weight of iron upon my head, and the bit in my mouth to keep me from speaking.

(D1v)

Although this 'device of containment' was 'never legitimate', the use of a 'cucking stool' was perfectly lawful. Also employed to punish 'scolds', a 'cucking stool' was 'a chair-like apparatus into which the offender was ordered strapped and then, to the jeers of the crowd, was dunked several times in water over her head' (Boose, 1991: 196, 185). As Boose concludes, the 'use and notoriety' of these devices were 'widespread enough for it to have been an agent in the historical production of women's silence' (197) through physical and psychological intimidation.

Paulina's reception at court does signal physical danger because when she insists on speaking, she is manhandled. Her lines, 'I pray you, do not push me' (2.3.124) and 'what needs these hands?' (2.3.126) are clear indications that she is being bodily threatened. The danger of physical abuse and its overhanging psychological effect has become manifest today whenever Black actresses have appraised the role. In the Black online magazine, *The Root*, Maisha Kai (2019) describes how the moment 'elicited audible responses' from the audience on the opening night when Christina Clark – a Black actress – played Paulina in a production of the play at Goodman Theatre because the line, 'what needs these hands?' is 'relatable to almost every woman in the audience – certainly, every black woman'. In a world in which Black women have regularly faced police brutality, the threat that a 'perceived' verbal misstep can attract violence from authority figures is distinctly palpable. Moreover, Clark explains how she, at least initially, worried about Paulina being interpreted as an 'angry black woman' (quoted in Kai, 2019), showing that the accusations such as 'mankind witch' have modern guises in epithets like 'angry black woman' which are similarly designed to disable. This chimes deeply with Boose's finding that physical tortures were linked with psychological ones through public shaming because 'the cucking of scolds was turned into a carnival experience, one that literally placed the woman's body at the centre of a mocking parade' (Boose, 1991: 189).

In *Hamlet*, the court's misogyny is not explicitly questioned but *The Winter's Tale* interrogates Leontes' attitude because Paulina 'maintains and consolidates her power in the second half of the play' (Belton, 2000: 160). As Ellen Belton argues, this power includes the right to public speech. As the play progresses, Leontes begins to trust and appreciate Paulina's words. For example, in 3.2, when Leontes thinks that his blameless wife is dead, he agrees that Paulina is right to berate him: 'Go on, go on. / Thou canst not speak too much; I have deserved / All tongues to talk their bitt'rest' (3.2.211–13). However, Paulina's speech continues to be challenged. Whereas Leontes might be converted, the other courtiers keep questioning Paulina's right to talk. In the same scene that Leontes urges Paulina to 'go on', a Lord recommends that she 'Say no more' (3.2.213). According to him, 'Howe'er the business goes, you have made fault / I'th'boldness of your speech' (3.2.213–15). This pattern is repeated in 5.1 when Paulina counsels Leontes against remarrying:

> If one by one you wedded all the world,
> Or from the all that are took something good
> To make the perfect woman, she you killed
> Would be unparalleled.

                                                            (5.1.13–16)

Leontes accepts Paulina's counsel but he recoils at her words:

> I think so. Killed!
> She I killed! I did so; but thou strik'st me
> Sorely to say I did. It is as bitter
> Upon thy tongue as in my thought. Now, good now,
> Say so but seldom.

                                                            (5.1.16–20)

Whether he is agreeing or disagreeing with Paulina, Leontes is still trying to dictate the limits of her speech when he requests her to 'say so but seldom'. A courtier, Cleomenes, however, jumps on this cue and tells Paulina that she should not say so 'at all' (5.1.20) and rebukes her that 'You might have spoken a thousand things that would / Have done the time more benefit, and graced / Your kindness better' (5.1.21–23).

In the final scene of the play in which Hermione's statue, as if miraculously, comes to life, Paulina, as Belton notes, starts to direct Leontes. 'I like your silence' (5.3.21), she first comments, but then she encourages him to 'speak' (5.3.22). Nonetheless, once Hermione, Perdita, and Leontes are reunited, Leontes makes another attempt to hush Paulina and it is worth noting the exact dialogue:

PAULINA: ... Go together
You precious winners all; your exultation
Partake to everyone. I, an old turtle,
Will wing me to some withered bough and there
My mate, that's never to be found again,
Lament till I am lost.
LEONTES: ... O peace, Paulina!
Thou shouldst a husband take by my consent

(5.3.130–36)

After insisting that Paulina stop talking and marry a husband of his choice, Leontes urges his courtier Camillo to 'take her by the hand' (5.3.144). This abrupt marriage and Leontes' choice of words has attracted much critical commentary. Michael Friedman (2002) has argued that Leontes propels Paulina 'towards marriage and its implied limitations on female speech ... Leontes negates Paulina's plans for a lonely but verbally independent retirement from the institution of matrimony by imposing on her a husband to manage her tongue' (226). This reading is strengthened if we look at Paulina's choice to 'lament'. A 'lament' was a genre or mode within complaint literature 'directed towards experiences of loss and grievance in diverse circumstances ... a stance of grief or protest in the face of loss or abandonment directed towards generating recognition and compassion in its audience' and it was a 'mode that women engaged with variously to make critical interventions in literary, political, and religious life across the early modern period' (Ross & Smith, 2020: 5, 21). Although, as Jennifer Richards and Alison Thorne (2007) point out, it is 'difficult for us nowadays properly to appreciate ... such apparently disabling yet pervasively used speech forms as supplication and complaint, which accentuated the speaker's lowliness, weakness and incapacity', female writers astutely used these forms as 'a highly effective vehicle for social and moral protest' (14, 16). Thus, by denying Paulina her right to lament, Leontes is also foreclosing the possibility of Paulina adopting a rhetorical mode through which to voice criticism. Taking an opposite view, Anna Kamaralli, argues that this line is not threatening because 'one thing that the play has repeatedly displayed is the abject failure of marriage to perform its prescribed task of curtailing the female tongue' (1131). While it is easy to imagine, with Kamaralli, that Paulina's tongue cannot be curtailed by matrimony, it is important not to overlook the detail that Leontes literally manages to silence Paulina at the end of this play by asking her to hold her peace and having the last word – a project that he began on Paulina's first entrance at his court.

1.3 The Acoustics of Shakespeare Studies

As the case-studies of Ophelia and Paulina demonstrate, Shakespeare's plays attest to the cost of silencing women; suppression of Ophelia's speech affects her mental health whereas not listening to Paulina has grave consequences for Leontes' court and life. More often than not, these plays implicitly or explicitly question this aural misogyny. At the very least, we, as educators, can use the plays to question and defy the gendered acoustic oppression exhibited in the worlds of the plays. So, it is disappointing that instead of disrupting these patterns, Shakespeare Studies tends to repeat them in different guises. Women Shakespeare scholars – both established and early-career ones – are frequently overlooked as speakers in public lectures and Shakespeare conference circuits. Let us take a few concrete examples from recent years.

The British Academy's Shakespeare Lectures is an annual lecture series and, since its inauguration in 1911, speakers have covered a range of subjects. However, even if we only count since the beginning of the twenty-first century until the most recent lecture (2000–18), the gender distribution is 13 men and 3 women.[23] Moreover, no woman of colour has yet been included in this series. Interestingly, the fund for this series was provided by a woman, Frida Mond, who, in her donation letter, specifically states that 'in order to emphasize the worldwide devotion to Shakespeare, any person, whether man or woman, of any nationality, shall be eligible to deliver the Shakespeare

---

[23] See: www.thebritishacademy.ac.uk/events/lectures/listings/shakespeare-lectures/.

oration' (Mond, quoted by British Academy, 2015: 52), thereby encouraging a sense of diversity that is not nurtured in the lecture series. A similar gender (im)balance is noticeable in the speakers at The Notre Dame London Shakespeare Lectures in honour of Professor Sir Stanley Wells. An annual lecture takes place as a part of this series at the London Global Gateway of the university and it has a pedagogic focus: 'envisioned as a celebration of a scholar of world renown, it is also a venue for students on the London program to meet leading academics and theatre practitioners who shape their fields'. Since its inception in 2012 to 2022, the series which has 'developed in close collaboration with the Shakespeare Birthplace Trust in Stratford-upon-Avon and the Shakespeare Institute (University of Birmingham)', has featured 7 men and 4 women. Again, no Black or Brown woman has been a speaker here.[24] The Kingston Shakespeare Seminar (KiSS), which promises to bring 'leading international Shakespeare scholars' to the Rose Theatre, Kingston-upon-Thames, hosts several lecture series, conferences, and colloquia.[25] Among these, the variously named Rose Shakespeare Lecture/ Shakespeare Birthday Lecture is an annual event that has exclusively featured men since 2014. Only 1 woman – a woman of colour – has given a lecture in this series in 2013. KiSS also runs a public lecture series on a more regular basis. Not counting the few lectures that are shared between participants, it has included 35 men and 11 women. The data for 2017 is particularly disheartening, with 8 public lectures by men and none by women.[26]

KiSS' bias also seeps into the conferences under aegis of The Kingston University. For example, it hosted the 'Shakespeare and Marlowe' conference in 2017 for which the gender breakdown of keynote speakers was 5 men and 1 woman, and it included a roundtable talk which comprised 4 men and 1 woman chaired by a man.[27] Some of the well-established conferences have also exhibited a similar prejudice. In 2013, The European Shakespeare Research Association's conference that takes place every two years welcomed

[24] See https://london.nd.edu/conferences-events/annual-shakespeare-lecture/.

[25] See https://kingstonshakespeareseminar.wordpress.com/about-2/.

[26] See https://kingstonshakespeareseminar.wordpress.com/past-events/.

[27] See www.kingston.ac.uk/events/item/2677/17-nov-2017-kingston-shakespeare-conference-marlowe-and-shakespeare/.

9 men and 3 women as plenary speakers and none of these were scholars of colour.[28] In 2014, the conference of the British Shakespeare Association (BSA) listed 1 woman and 4 men as plenary speakers, with 2 of the men sharing the stage as part of a conversation. Neither of these plenary speakers was a person of colour.[29] In 2016, the BSA's conference included 3 women and 5 men as keynote speakers and none of these were women of colour.[30] In the same year, as I noted in the Introduction, the underrepresentation of women as plenary speakers disappointed the participants of the World Shakespeare Congress. When academics pointed this out on Twitter, they were offered reasons such as women were unavailable or unsuitable.[31] This statement is telling because, as *Jezebel*'s tongue-in-cheek 'Female Conference Speaker Bingo' – a 'bingo card full of excuses for not having more female speakers' – attests, statements such as 'all the women were probably busy' or 'we need big-name speakers, and few of those are women' are staple explanations that are given by organizers when they are questioned on the lack of gender parity.[32] It is interesting to consider these figures in the light of opportunities that young women and/or Early-Career women scholars have for presenting their work beyond the conferences that are specifically aimed at postgraduates. Only the Shakespeare Association of America seems to reserve a slot for the next generation of scholars.

The data presented here is patchy and reflects the partial nature of such records in the public domain. So, I do not wish to give the impression that there have *never* been conferences that have disrupted this trend. The 2019 BSA conference is a case in point as all plenary speakers at this event were

---

[28] See www.um.es/shakespeare/esra/conferences/documentos/shakespeare-and-myth_programme-at-a-glance.pdf.

[29] See www.shakespeare.stir.ac.uk/wp-content/uploads/2013/03/BSA2014-Full-Programme19June.pdf.

[30] See www.britishshakespeare.ws/bsa-news/reports-from-the-hull-bsa-conference/.

[31] For example, see https://twitter.com/DrSarahOlive/status/760838266656436224 or https://twitter.com/alhegland/status/760850024616038400.

[32] This card was first introduced by the feminist online magazine, *Jezebel*, in 2012 but it is no longer available there. Instead it is reproduced on the *Gender Avenger* website here: www.genderavenger.com/blog/2014/2/25/an-oldie-but-a-goodie-jezebels-female-conference-speaker-bingo.

women of colour. However, the very fact that I have been able to collect multiple instances in which major conferences and lecture series have marginalized women in the twenty-first century itself speaks to the gender disparity in the public voice of Shakespeare scholarship. Since, as Lennon points out, conferences can be seen as 'pockets and examples of higher education' or 'a microcosm of the bigger problem',[33] these examples typify the (often unconscious) systemic bias against women's public voices in Shakespeare Studies.

The acoustics of the conferences and lecture circuits, in turn, influence students' perception of the discipline. My students found these statistics unsettling and, in Sound 1, which accompanies this Element, they describe how these patterns at conferences and public lectures were disturbing to them.

Sound 1 Classroom Discussion: Audio file available at www.cambridge.org/panjwani.

For instance, as Natassja Singh's remark in the clip indicates, she felt that this is indicative of a 'whole mentality still that just 'cause we open our mouths and we're allowed to go to education, that doesn't mean we should be able to say stuff and I think that's ridiculous'. While Singh thought that such disparities make women feel like outsiders in the education system, Stella Khue Nguyen and Elizabeth Triscari respectively elaborate why it was a particular concern for Humanities in general and Shakespeare Studies in particular:

> NGUYEN: The thing that really stood out to me after I looked at the data that you've given is that women have always been framed as the ones that dominate Humanities. Even looking at this classroom, women dominate the classroom, but then the people [who] are considered professionals

---

[33] Personal Communication, Informal Interview, January 2022.

or leaders of the field and get to speak their opinion, are mostly men.

TRISCARI: My first thought is that it sets a standard for just in academia in general and with Shakespeare whose work is so deeply ingrained in what we believe in Western society is 'intelligence' and 'scholarly'. [The speaker lists] are a representation just of how male academics think of female ones and how much they respect them or rather don't respect them. And it's sort of a boys' club where there shouldn't be a boys' club, you know?

The bias has profound ramifications for men in the classroom too as Zeke Tweedie explains in the clip:

I think that from a man's perspective, there's a drawback as well, even though, obviously, it's not as serious as the negative effect of it all on women ... from a man's perspective, we're kind of stuck in this echo chamber of listening to people who have our own experiences talk about Shakespeare so we are suffering from not being able to hear the opinions of people who are coming from a different experience. To be honest, there's at least a half dozen times in this class alone where we pointed something out that I wouldn't really have noticed otherwise, just because I'm not really able to read Ophelia in the same way that women are. So, if I had to go to a class with a White male professor and read articles and watch lectures by White guys, I'd obviously be missing out on a lot.

1.4 'I'm speaking! I'm speaking!': Podcasts as Cyberfeminism

Podcasts have proved attractive to women and minoritized scholars and practitioners in the field. Brown (2021) uses podcasts to introduce the voices of scholars from racial minorities as part of his anti-racist pedagogy. One of the reasons that these voices feature on podcasts at all might be because the consumers of podcasts value aural diversity. This trend differs significantly from mainstream listening practices which, as the introduction to this section outlined, are based on a sonic culture which privileges White and male voices. As Mottram's (2016) study concludes, 'due to the nature of the medium, vocal authority may be qualified differently in podcasting than in other communication mediums. Finding vocal authority in podcasts is not about achieving the traditional Western aesthetic of the low, deep voice, but about sounding like a "real" person: individually authentic' (66). As a result, podcasting culture is amenable to voices that are not mainstream or traditionally considered authoritative, thereby creating a more encouraging reception for diverse women's public speech with different accents, dialects, and vocal textures.

Moreover, unlike conference keynotes and plenaries or public lecture speaker engagements, podcasts are not dependent on invitations from organizations and institutions, and can still reach wide audiences. Sean Richardson and Heather Green (2018) employ podcasts for feminist pedagogy. Examining the 'multifaceted feminist potentiality of podcasting', they suggest that podcasts can be an advantageous alternative to in-person conferences which have 'intersectional implications for women scholars: performance anxiety and imposter syndrome, emotional labor and caring responsibilities, harassment, and accessibility issues surrounding which bodies can(not) engage with conference spaces'. So, podcasts can 'help scholars circumnavigate certain tensions, especially in respect to spatial and temporal constraints … because podcast hosts and panellists are able to record themselves from their own home, using phones, laptops, Dictaphones or other devices' (285). This is also the cheaper option in most cases. For their economic accessibility, podcasting has been compared to the 'Shakespearean-era print market'. Just as 'parallel advancements of forms of literacy and access and cost of materials' (Kimbro, Noschka, & Way, 2019: 5) made print financially viable and desirable in the sixteenth and seventeenth centuries, advancements in both media literacy and cost of materials make podcasting an attractive option for distributing work in the twenty-first century. 'Many home computing products come pre-loaded with the equipment one might need to record and distribute a podcast (notwithstanding quality control of sound, etc.). Podcast hosting fees for the amateur are cheap, oftentimes free for a limited period' (Kimbro, Noschka, & Way, 2019: 5). At the user end, too, podcasts are more accessible for the same reasons and because they are 'usually distributed as part of a freemium model: there is no charge for the core product' (Spinelli & Dann, 2019: 8).

Perhaps this is why the acoustics of the Shakespeare podverse are different from the soundscape of Shakespeare conferences and lectures. If plenary speakers are the most prominent voices at such events, then it is the hosts who are important in podcasts because they are the ones whose voices the listeners hear and bond with in every episode. So, it is promising that women feature prominently as host speakers for both independent and institutionally affiliated podcasts. The Folger Shakespeare Library, for instance, produces the *Shakespeare Unlimited* podcast. Each of its episodes features guests and, after a short introduction by Michael Witmore, they are interviewed either by Barbara Bogaev or Neva Grant or Rebecca Sheir. The podcast creators have also invited a number of women scholars to address not only women-centred Shakespeare subjects but also textual, performance, editorial, architectural, social, cultural, and culinary history of Shakespeare.[34] Similarly, the *Such Stuff* podcast from Shakespeare's Globe is closely tied to the work of this institution and has an avowed commitment to looking at 'Shakespeare's transformative impact on the world around us, asking questions about programming, gender, race, social justice and their relationship to Shakespeare'. It takes the form of discussions and interviews and is hosted by Michelle Terry, Farah Karim-Cooper, and Imogen Greenberg.[35] The *Women & Shakespeare* podcast, which I host, is structured as conversations exclusively with diverse women creatives and academics.[36] Employing a different format, Emma Smith ran a highly successful podcast series, *Approaching Shakespeare*, in the form of lectures which she recorded in her classroom at The University of Oxford.[37] Alternatively, *The Hurly Burly Shakespeare Show!* is an 'an irreverent mix of entertainment and scholarly content' and takes the form of conversations between Jess Hamlet and Aubrey Whitlock with additional guests for some episodes.[38] Stephanie

---

[34] www.folger.edu/shakespeare-unlimited.

[35] www.shakespearesglobe.com/such-stuff-podcast/.

[36] http://womenandshakespeare.com/.

[37] https://podcasts.ox.ac.uk/series/approaching-shakespeare.

[38] https://hurlyburlyshakespeareshow.com/.

Crugnola's *Protest Too Much* is playful and innovative in pitting the 'host against performers, educators, and scholars in a battle' about Shakespeare's characters. The guests argue which of Shakespeare's characters would win the title of the 'best' friend, villain, lover, overall personality, and so on and they also nominate a (seemingly indefensible) character that the host has to support. The informal debates that this structure generates challenge conventional readings of Shakespeare's characters.[39] *Let Him Roar Again* explores Shakespeare in the rehearsal room and the classroom in an Australian context and is hosted by actor and drama teacher, Amy Perry.[40] To mention just three more, Cassidy Cash's *That Shakespeare Life!* focuses on 'the history of the man' and interviews 'the history experts who know Shakespeare best',[41] *The Play's the Thing* dedicates six episodes to each Shakespeare play and is hosted by two women (Heidi White and Sarah-Jane Bentley) and one man (Tim McIntosh),[42] and *Not Another Shakespeare Podcast!*, which declares that it 'takes neither itself nor Shakespeare seriously', is hosted by the couple Nora Williams and James Platt and, in a tongue-in-cheek rebuke to patriarchal descriptions, bills Nora as the 'theatre nerd/Shax expert' and James as 'husband/theatre sceptic'.[43] It is also noteworthy that these women are at different stages in their careers from professors at well-established higher education institutions to early-career academics to adjunct lecturers to performers, to school teachers, to illustrators, and film-makers. They also come from diverse backgrounds and possess a variety of accents and voice qualities.

This list is not meant to indicate that there are no Shakespeare podcasts which are hosted by men or that podcasts have solved the issue of women not being handed the mic in our field. Rather, it is an example of cyberfeminism that has the potential to change the aural landscape of Shakespeare pedagogy because the affordances of this technology are making it possible to create spaces that do not currently exist in the offline world. However,

---

[39] http://protesttoomuch.com/.
[40] https://lethimroaragain.com/podcast-episodes/.
[41] www.cassidycash.com/thatshakespearelife/.
[42] https://shows.acast.com/the-plays-the-thing.
[43] https://anchor.fm/nashaxpodcast/.

the existence of podcasts should not preclude a call for fairness in the conference circuit. On her blog, Jacqueline Wernimont (2015) produced a crowdsourced list of women 'who can be invited as featured or plenary speakers' when she saw a similar gendered marginalization in the DH conferences and declared that 'going forward, all-male panels can only be construed as a choice, not an issue of ignorance. We have been busy building communities we want to see in DH, and now we've taken the time from our own research, our teaching, our lives to pull together information for you – now it's your turn to do your part'. Similarly, these podcasts are audio lists of potential conference speakers but they are also more than that. Together, they constitute a virtual space which models the kind of soundscape that our students want and need in Shakespeare Studies. By existing as spaces where women are 'featured' speakers they beg the question of why such spaces do not exist offline too and can be used to argue for more equity in the sector. They are cyberfeminist ways of showing the positive impact that hearing diverse women's voices can have on our students if we utilize such podcasts in our teaching. Investing in the interrogation of the existing offline soundscape, promoting the amplification of women experts, and practicing the feminist teaching facilitated by such women-led podcasts is participating in feminist Shakespeare podagogy. A former student, Apurva Kothari, writes that listening to the voices of women speaking about Shakespeare 'is particularly useful for me, as it makes me feel that Shakespeare is for me and people like me. Furthermore, I do feel that Shakespeare continues to hold substantial cultural capital, so it is important to know, especially as a student, how women are mobilising Shakespeare to create more empowering cultures for women themselves' (Kothari, 2021: 6). Just as Woolf argued in *A Room of One's Own*, witnessing a tradition of women writers would be powerful for women who subsequently sought to put pen to paper, for Kothari, auditing a tradition of women speaking on Shakespeare sanctioned her own engagement with the playwright.

Perhaps making and using podcasts in a predominantly silencing culture feels like a very insignificant and inadequate solution. Reflecting on queer feminist media praxis in the online journal *Ada*, Alexandra Juhasz (2014) also captures this feeling. 'In my experience, the making and living of alternative, counter or radical culture, through media praxis, does not feel fully revolutionary in its own time because each act of making is too small, unstable, marginal, and precarious; the dominant culture, and its media praxis, looms large, solid, and powerful'. Yet she suggests that 'each of these risky acts makes not just media that lasts for future study (and sometimes consolidation as a movement) but small, beautiful, fleeting instants of potential – "revolutionary-instants" – that we recognize and celebrate mostly in their doing and living'. In 2020, a Black student participated in creating one of the podcast episodes of *Women & Shakespeare*. This episode features a Black British author who adapted *Julius Caesar* to talk about child soldiers in Sierra Leone and edited the essay collection *Shakespeare, Race and Performance* (Jarrett-Macauley, 2020). Listening to a Black woman scholar shape Shakespeare for her own use and taking part in the creation of the podcast made my student realize that she could 'own Shakespeare' so much so that she applied to graduate school to pursue further studies in Shakespeare even though she had had an 'unsure relationship with Shakespeare'[44] before she got involved in the podcast. Perhaps this small result is a good start.

2 Record: Building Podcast Archives with Shakespeare Actresses

Doña Croll played Nerissa in the 1987 production of *The Merchant of Venice* at the Royal Exchange Theatre, Manchester. In a *Women & Shakespeare* podcast episode, she remembers what happened in rehearsals:

> When I played Nerissa . . . the director said to me, 'I think Nerissa is a bit older and wiser than Portia. And I think Portia gets a lot of this' and he showed me what he meant. He put one hand on his hip and the other and his right finger, he wagged in my face. Of course, what I saw and heard was 'Aw miss Portia' [in a stereotypical 'mammy' accent] . . . And I'm not doing that! So, I never did it once. And what

[44] Personal Communication, email, 16 September 2020.

I did was so much more interesting, so much more layered,
and textured, and human. So much better than he'd ever
imagined that he never gave me a note.

(Croll, 2020)

This account illustrates how Croll's embodied experience of both working
as an actress of colour in UK and playing Shakespeare roles meant that she
could recognize and defy the director's lazy racial stereotype and his narrow
understanding of Nerissa. So, if we do not have access to such interviews
then we will not be able to appreciate an actress' personal and analytical
input in creating a 'layered, and textured, and human' interpretation of
a character such as Nerissa.

Actresses' accounts of a role are useful not only in tracking their resistance to
directors' decisions but also in mapping their differences with reviewers' critiques. For instance, in his review of Adrian Noble's 1985 Royal Shakespeare
Company (RSC) production of *As You Like It* for *Shakespeare Quarterly*, Roger
Warren records the staging of a 'hunting episode' in which, instead of killing
a deer as the play indicates, 'Jaques drew a bloodstained sheet across [Celia] as
she slept, and the lords then pursued her around the stage as if she were the
hunted deer'. Warren (1986) interprets this as Celia's 'erotic dream' or 'sexual
awakening'. This disturbing and predatory staging is lauded by Warren when he
opines that this was the production's 'clearest idea' and that 'Fiona Shaw's Celia
gains' from it (11). That Warren's observations are uncritically repeated in the
RSC edition of the play demonstrates how production histories crystallize
around reviewers' judgements (Brown & Sewell, 2010: 128–9). However, in
two detailed accounts of her role discussed later in this section, Shaw never once
alludes to this staging which (at least to me) reads as gratuitous rape dramaturgy.
Shaw writes a different performance history and preserves a divergent memory
of the production's strengths. In this case, Shaw's insight is necessary to provide
a counter-performance history written from the actress' point of view.

Making a case for studying performers' analysis of their roles, Philip
Brockbank (1989) writes that 'readers and theatre-goers, whether critical or
uncritical, ignorant or informed, have dominated the history of
Shakespearean commentary, and actors have commonly had more opportunity to read about their own performances than to write about them'. He

elaborates that their reflections are an untapped resource because actors have 'read and sometimes assiduously studied the plays and parts they acted, and they know better than most students or onlookers that a Shakespearean play is the sum of many possible readings and many possible performances' (1). Increasingly, Shakespeare scholarship and education are beginning to pay attention to performers' views as evinced by conversations with Shakespeare performers in databases such as *Digital Theatre +* and *Drama Online*,[45] a whole section on practitioner interviews and reflections curated by C. K. Ash and Nora J. Williams in *The Arden Research Handbook of Shakespeare and Contemporary Performance* (Kirwan & Prince, 2021), book-length studies such as *Brutus and Other Heroines* (Walter, 2016) and *Performing Shakespeare's Women* (Reynolds, 2018), the 'Players of Shakespeare' series which was conceived to give authoritative voice to Shakespearean actors, and the RSC editions of Shakespeare's plays that have taken steps to redress the scarcity of commentary from creatives by including discussions with Shakespeare performers and directors. However, conversations with and reflections by actresses are still proportionately scarce. Despite Carol Rutter's (1988) germinal work in this field, few have followed in her footsteps systematically. Pascale Aebischer points out how the 'Players of Shakespeare' series has a gender bias. While researching *Othello* and *Titus Andronicus*, she found that the series contained 'articles by actors of Titus, Othello, and Iago, but allows no actress playing the roles of Lavinia, Tamora, Desdemona, or Emilia to express her opinion of the role'. This predisposition was mirrored by reviewers who, too, 'have a tendency to interview the director and actors responsible for the parts of Othello and Iago' so much so that Aebischer (1999) could not find 'a single interview with an actress in all the reviews of the productions of *Othello* that [she had] access to' (41). This propensity is not unique to *Othello* because across its six volumes, the 'Players of Shakespeare' series includes essays by 22 actresses which is less than half the number of those by actors who have penned 54 articles for this series. Of these 22, there is no woman of colour,

---

[45] Both databases are behind a paywall but information about them is available here: www.digitaltheatreplus.com/about, www.dramaonlinelibrary.com/about-drama-online.

and there is very little commentary by actresses who have played relatively minor (albeit significant) parts whereas actors who have played roles like Launcelot Gobbo in *The Merchant of Venice* or Autolycus in *The Winter's Tale* have been allowed to reflect on the significance of these seemingly small parts. If Aebischer were writing after the publication of the RSC edition of *Othello*, she would have met with the same roadblock because it too contains two interviews by male directors and an interview with an actor who has played Iago but no interviews of actresses who have played either Desdemona or Emilia. Following this pattern, the editions of other plays in the series including *Antony and Cleopatra*, *Coriolanus*, *Macbeth*, *The Tempest*, *Twelfth Night*, *A Midsummer Night's Dream*, the joint edition of *Titus Andronicus* and *Timon of Athens*, *The Two Gentlemen of Verona*, *All's Well that Ends Well*, *Henry IV Part I*, *Henry IV Part II*, *Henry V*, *Henry VI Parts I, II, III*, *Richard III*, and *Cymbeline* contain interviews exclusively with male directors, actors, and designers. The editions of *Hamlet* and *The Winter's Tale* make space for interviews with 3 male directors each but do not include interviews of actresses who have played Ophelia or Paulina – the two characters that I discussed in Section 1.

Therefore, the first two parts of this section argue that we need an archive of actresses' insights into playing Shakespeare because not having access to such conversations skews our students' understanding of women's roles in Shakespeare's plays and adds to the hegemonic concentration on male roles in Shakespeare criticism. Moreover, it both diminishes the embodied experiences that actresses bring to bear in their interpretation of the roles and effaces their 'labor, agency, and craft' (Henderson, 2006: 78) even as it privileges the (often male) directors' ideas.[46] It also leaves little room for counter-memories or opposing performance histories that are brought to light if we pay attention to actresses' analysis and rehearsal experience of their roles. So, I am making the case for what Maryanne Dever (quoting Sheffield) calls 'archival activism' and 'archival

---

[46] Henderson is not making a gendered argument here nor is she talking specifically about actresses' embodied knowledge. However, she is urging a move away from the auteurist model of reading a production which often focusses on the director only and towards a more collaborative understanding in which all creatives contribute

interventions', that is, 'using research and documentation to create an archive where one does not already exist' (Sheffield quoted in Dever, 2017: 3). I do so through my experience of teaching two plays: *The Merchant of Venice* and *As You Like It*.[47] While studying these plays, my students and I came up against the sparseness of material that we wanted. For example, the RSC edition of *The Merchant of Venice* finds room for 4 interviews – 2 with male directors and 2 with actors who have played Shylock – but does not contain conversations with actresses who have played Portia, Nerissa, or Jessica and while the edition of *As You Like It* does have an interview with an actress who played Rosalind, the actresses who have performed Celia are overlooked even though there are 2 interviews with male directors of the play. However, nuanced feminist readings of the plays emerged when we managed to find actresses' accounts of playing Portia, Jessica, and Celia and interpreted the plays through the prism of their thoughts.

The final part of this section posits that podcasting technology can aid in building archives and recording interviews, conversations, anecdotes, and reflections by Shakespeare actresses. By recording, I mean both that especially commissioned interviews and conversations can be generated and spoken words converted into more permanent and portable sound formats such as MP3 or .wav but I also mean that podcasts can act as online spaces where such conversations are housed and made available to present and future generations; podcasting can combine the functions of production and archiving. While Section 1 concentrated on the amplifying feature of podcasting, this section elaborates why the 'intrinsic archival potential' (Hogan, 2008: 200) of podcasts might be suited to aiding Shakespeare Studies in building this rich performance history resource that can make our Shakespeare pedagogy feminist.

---

[47] Unless otherwise noted, all in-text citations of *The Merchant of Venice* are from W. Shakespeare, *The Merchant of Venice*, J. Bate and E. Rasmussen, eds. London: Macmillan, 2010 and all in-text citations of *As You Like It* are from W. Shakespeare, *As You Like It*, M. Hattaway, ed. Cambridge: Cambridge University Press, 2009.

2.1 Teaching Intersectional Feminism with The Merchant of Venice

In the post-Holocaust world, 'the performance history of *The Merchant of Venice* has been dominated by the figure of Shylock' (Brown & Kirwan, 2010: 115), declares the RSC edition of the play before commencing on a detailed performance history of the play which centres on Shylock. In other words, the edition reinforces the traditional performance history narrative rather than disrupting or challenging it. This tendency has rankled feminist critics such as Rosemary Gaby who observes that 'directors and their male stars wrestle with the problem of Shylock for a whole host of politically laudable reasons, but they often still do so within structures that make it all too easy to forget who has the most lines' (quoted in Gay, 2002: 453), alluding to the fact that Portia speaks 22% of the lines, making hers the biggest speaking part in the play.[48] In response to Gaby's comments, Penny Gay (2002) not only writes a detailed performance history of Portia in twentieth-century English theatre but also presents her as a figurehead for feminism when she argues that 'no other of Shakespeare's plays leaves us with the image of such a powerful and self-determined woman' or when she describes her as a 'woman who has reserves of intellect and dignity which will protect her from anything that the patriarchy and chance combined may impose on her' (431). Taking my cue from these critics, when I was teaching *The Merchant of Venice*, I was determined to include Portia in our discussions.

We began by looking at Portia's most powerful public utterances which occur in the courtroom drama of 4.1 where, dressed as a young lawyer Balthazar, she intercedes between Antonio and Shylock. Even before my students read the play, they were aware of Portia's 'The quality of mercy is not strained' (4.1.190–211) speech which continues to hold significant cultural capital. Some of them had also seen famous British actors such as Judi Dench, Jade Anouka, Harriet Walter, and Meera Syal sharing the speech between them in a video that went viral during the COVID-19 pandemic.[49] Anyone studying, performing, or watching the play pays

---

[48] See the Key Facts section of the RSC edition, 18.

[49] www.youtube.com/watch?v=VcsdZieco14. It is interesting that part of the speech's sheer force is derived from its composition. This would require the kind of rhetorical

attention to it, but it is not only these lines but the entire scene that influences the interpretation of Portia. The legal wrangling and Portia's idea that no drop of Antonio's blood should be spilled in extracting the pound of flesh which Shylock demands is a much-negotiated turning point in performance. As Gay (2002) observes, an actress taking on the role must decide whether this quibble is 'a well-prepared piece of courtroom histrionics, or a genuine flash of desperate inspiration' (431). In order to discover the different performance choices, my students and I started by collating actresses' accounts of playing Portia.

For Deborah Findlay (1993) who played Portia in 1987, this was the question around which a tug of war occurred in rehearsals (62–5). Antony Sher, a South-African Jewish actor, who played Shylock to Findlay's Portia, explained that by the trial scene, his Shylock had been so 'badly damaged by his treatment' that he was 'insane with rage' and this mental state was intensified in performance by 'having him perform a (totally invented) Jewish ritual while he prepared to cut the pound of flesh from Antonio' (Sher, 2010: 165). The RSC website details that this involved 'washing each hand three times and dripping three drops of blood from a horn while intoning the *Shefoch Chamatcha*, an actual Hebrew text recited at the Passover when a cup is drunk to Elijah, invoking him to punish the tormentors of Israel'. This Shylock was prepared for his revenge on the antisemitic Christians who, in turn, were reciting the Lord's prayer in Latin in this production.[50] However, far from merely showing Shylock's mental state, Findlay (1993: 63) explains that this ritual was meant to suggest that Portia gets the idea that no drop of blood should be spilled in extracting the pound of flesh from Antonio when she watches Shylock dripping blood from this horn. Findlay admits that due to this dramaturgy, at first, she 'started out thinking that Portia is naïve enough to come into the trial with only the conviction that

training in public speaking that, as I describe in Section 1, humanist scholars such as Vives and Brathwait considered unnecessary for a woman in Shakespeare's time. So, in this play Shakespeare creates a privileged heroine who seems to have received learning that is not hindered by gendered educational precepts.

[50] See www.rsc.org.uk/the-merchant-of-venice/past-productions/bill-alexander-1987-production.

she can convince Shylock to be merciful' and after that fails, 'she is acting on her wits'. However, Findlay decided that 'this was to undervalue' Portia. She eventually felt that, in the play, 'Portia is in control of the scene from the moment she enters … she *does* have all the alternatives when she comes into the trial. Rather than being fed the solution by Shylock *she* runs the scene' and 'follows a simple rule of thumb: mercy, or justice' (63, 63–4). She offers Shylock 'as many chances as she can to choose mercy, but once he has made his choice … she follows the consequences through to their final terrible conclusion. Hers is an act of strict impartiality, explaining the law to everyone present'. However, staging the ritual made it impossible to sustain this 'momentum of Portia's logic' and, according to Findlay, it 'meant playing the scene in a bewildered state, buffeted by the events and grabbing onto the solution in a last desperate attempt' (64, 63). Tellingly, she writes that even though she knew that this ritual was doing a disservice to Portia's power and speeches in this scene, she did not try to get this cut because she 'was not man enough' (64) to challenge the actor and director's version.

This turning point was important for Sinead Cusack, too, when she played Portia in the 1981 production, directed by John Barton, who was apparently 'concerned to "re-balance" the play, in response to new feminist criticism, in favour of Portia' (quoted in Gay, 2002: 442). Cusack (1989) was also convinced that, as Portia, 'when I entered the courtroom I knew exactly how to save Antonio'. However, she explains that the reason that her Portia did not activate this clause straightaway was because 'she doesn't go into the courtroom to save Antonio (that's easy) but to save Shylock, to redeem him – she is passionate to do that. She gives him opportunity after opportunity to relent and to exercise his humanity' (39). However, just like in the production with Findlay, Cusack explains that due to the director's way of working and rehearsing actors in isolation or pairs, the staging of the relationship between Portia's newlywed husband Bassanio and his friend Antonio 'was kept from [her] until a very late stage in rehearsal'. She discovered that while Shylock and Portia were discussing the finer points of law and justice, 'there was an undressing process going on downstage right, between Antonio and Bassanio, which was riveting in its detail. Collar studs and buttons were being undone, all in mime of course, and there was a lot of kissing' (37). She describes how she felt that with this going on downstage, her Portia 'didn't have a chance' (39) to hold the audience. Her language echoes Findlay's – just as Findlay had felt that she 'was not man enough' to challenge the stagecraft, Cusack says that 'I didn't have the courage' (37) to oppose this dramaturgy.

In contrast, Walter, who was Portia in the same production in which Croll played Nerissa, thought that Portia's idea was 'a brainwave, unlooked-for and unplanned'. Her Portia's agenda was to 'prove beyond doubt that Shylock will carry out his bond to its logical end' (Walter, 2016: 34, 33). While she takes the opposite approach, in her version, too, Portia is a consummate lawyer who might not have everything sketched out but knows that she needs to prove to the court that her opponent was given every opportunity to resolve the matter amicably and therefore, upon his refusal to accept any of the terms, deserves the damages imposed upon him. Kathryn Pogson, who played Portia in the opening season of Shakespeare's Globe in 1998 also thinks that Portia would have the required knowledge and skill before entering the courtroom. She elaborates that a male disguise affords Portia the opportunity to 'really sit within the confidence of her own intelligence. And an intelligence that doesn't have to be defended because it's going to be listened to' (Pogson, 2020). Walter's feelings of playing this scene were similar and she, too, describes how she 'felt the disconcerting thrill of power' in this scene. She 'enjoyed it, felt ashamed of it, felt jealous of [her] male counterparts . . . Like Portia [she] had a moment's insight into what it was to be a man' (Walter, 2016: 35). So, Walter, Findlay, Cusack, and Pogson all agree with Gay's assessment that Shakespeare has written a heroine whose intelligence and 'public eloquence is carefully set up' (Gay, 2002: 432) right from the beginning and the male disguise simply affords her the opportunity to experience 'the masculine power of authoritative speech – that is, speech that a representative sector of (male-defined) society will listen to with respect' (431): speech that will have a powerful impact on laws and social structure.

After they had engaged with these actresses' reflections, my students were unanimous in their conviction that, due to their embodied knowledge of what it is to be a woman in a man's world and their astute textual analysis of the role, actresses such as Findlay and Cusack should have had more agency in shaping their performances. Although admitting that the pressures being described here were of a different nature and degree, Student A was quick to make a link between these oppressive accounts and the #MeToo movement which, they said, 'exposed the abuse of the power that male directors exercise in rehearsal rooms'.[51] However, they were also troubled by Portia as a character after encountering these readings. Student B did not agree that Portia's 'rule of thumb: mercy, or justice' is that 'simple' and insisted that perhaps it was better for the audience to focus on Shylock to see how damaged he is and understand why he is in no state to respond to pleas of mercy that he has not been shown but is expected to show. They also disagreed that this was a 'strict act of impartiality' as Findlay had put it. They were particularly uncomfortable with Cusack's idea of Portia trying to 'save Shylock' and punishing him when he refuses to be redeemed by Portia (whom he perceives as a Christian man, Balthazar). 'What *is* this if not White saviour complex?' posed Student C (original emphasis), aligning Portia's perceived stance to Teju Cole's claim that 'the White savior industrial complex is not about justice. It is about having a big emotional experience that validates privilege' or about satisfying the 'sentimental needs' of White people while acting as redeemers (Cole, 2012). Once this idea was raised, students contended that Portia can be interpreted as either a lawyer who wants to prove beyond doubt that Shylock is unremitting (as Walter suggests) or wants to be a saviour (as Cusack claims). In either case, however, they agreed with Hall (1992) that it is significant to register that Portia's 'strongest verbal abilities are only bent toward supporting a status quo which mandates the repulsion of aliens and outsiders' (104).

These thoughts also led them to re-examine the early scenes between Portia and the foreign dignitaries – Aragon and Morocco – who come to her house in Belmont to try the casket test that Portia's late father had set to determine Portia's husband. In Barton's production, Cusack (1989) describes how both these foreigners circled the women 'like animals getting ready to pounce' (34). In Bill Alexander's production, Findlay (1993) explicates:

---

[51] I have anonymized students' names if I have not been able to obtain their explicit permission to quote them.

> We felt that Morocco would treat a wife as his property,
> appropriate her physically, so there was a bit of manhand-
> ling in the scene which Portia reacted against. This may
> have been seen as reacting against his colour but it is much
> more to do with being treated as a sexual object – an
> interesting conundrum: who is the oppressor?

She asserts that 'rather than racial politics I think the scenes are about sexual politics' (59). However, thanks to increased awareness about false rape allegations brought against Black men, it was apparent to the students that both productions' performance choices were reinforcing or exaggerating the text's stereotyping and racial profiling of Black men as sexual predators.[52] Hall (1992) has contended that the 'imagery associated with Shylock in the play reveals an ongoing link between perceptions of racial difference of the black, the religious difference of the Jew, and the possible ramifications of sexual and economic contact with both. We can clearly see how the discourses of Otherness coalesce in the language of the play' (100). Thus, Portia's attitude towards Morocco buttresses the interpretation of her attitude towards Shylock. This understanding forced the students to examine the role of White women both within and outside the play in aligning themselves with structures of racism and antisemitism – a reading which was aided by the casting choices of these productions. They began to see Portia as a complex character who might be a victim of patriarchy but is also a perpetrator of other social injustices. Moreover, due to Findlay's and the production's pitting of racism and antisemitism against sexism, the students arrived at a crucial question – 'can Portia be racist, antisemitic and yet a feminist?'

To confront this question, I encouraged students to turn to Portia's interaction with another character in the play who is both Jewish and a woman: Jessica. She is not mentioned in either Findlay's or Cusack's

---

[52] Most of them had seen the 2019 Netflix series *When They See Us*, which reanimated the conversation around the 1989 Central Park Five case in which five teenagers (four Black and one Latinx) were arrested and wrongfully convicted in connection with the rape and assault of a White female jogger.

accounts perhaps because there is only one instance where Jessica and Portia address each other directly:

JESSICA: I wish your ladyship all heart's content.
PORTIA: I thank you for your wish, and am well pleased
            To wish it back on you: fare you well Jessica.

                                                    (3.4.44–45).

Polite exchanges such as these perhaps led Walter (2016) to insist that Portia 'shows no racist hostility' to Jessica 'contrary to what has sometimes been suggested' (30). However, Portia is never *openly* hostile to anyone, including the Prince of Morocco, whom she calls 'renowned prince' (2.1.20) and 'fair' (2.1.20) to his face before declaring 'let all of his complexion choose me so' (2.8.80) as soon as his back is turned.[53] More than this polite exchange, then, the fact that Portia leaves the newly-married Jessica and Lorenzo in charge of Belmont when she goes on her Venetian sojourn might indicate that she is welcoming to Jessica who, having eloped by dressing as a boy, has escaped the patriarchal tyranny of Shylock. At first, Portia's support of the married couple seems to indicate her commitment to feminist sisterhood. However, a crucial point that cannot be overlooked is that Jessica has converted to Christianity and is married to the Christian Lorenzo at this point – a fact that is stated several times in this text. In other words, there is no doubt that Jessica has 'divorce[d] herself from her Jewish ancestry' (Hall, 1992: 102) and has assimilated into the dominant culture by the time she meets Portia.

Jessica's conversion is 'potentially the most damning action to modern sensibilities' (Middleton, 2015: 297) because it is read as a betrayal of her religion on her part. However, this is a world in which 'aliens must be either

---

[53] Many editors and directors insist that in this line Portia could be objecting to Morocco's qualities rather than skin colour because the word 'complexion' could mean temperament/skin colour. However, the context makes it clear that it is Morocco's skin colour that is under discussion. Morocco himself refers to his 'complexion' and 'hue' which, he explains, is different due to sunburn. For more on the way in which sunburn operated as a trope through which racial difference could be negotiated, see Hall, 1995, pp. 92–107.

assimilated into the dominant culture (Shylock's and Jessica's conversions) and/or completely disempowered (Shylock's sentence)' (Hall, 1992: 101–2). This presents a difficulty for Jessica who, at the beginning of the play, is both alienated from the dominant culture as she is Jewish and trapped with her overbearing father as a woman in a patriarchal household. To understand Jessica's unique position, we turned to the 'intersectionality' framework developed by Kimberlé Crenshaw. This was a word that a lot of the students had encountered before but they now heard Crenshaw's TED talk with attentive ears when she explained that she had to develop this framework to 'deal with the fact that many of our social justice problems like racism and sexism are often overlapping, creating multiple levels of social injustice' for people at the intersection of these categories. Crenshaw (2016) offers the example of an African-American woman who was being discriminated against in the hiring policies of a car manufacturing firm because 'the African-Americans that were hired, usually for industrial jobs, maintenance jobs, were all men. And the women that were hired, usually for secretarial or front-office work, were all White'. Yet the court was not entertaining the woman's complaint because, in the eyes of the law, the manufacturer was neither discriminating against gender, nor race. By using this framework, students were able to see critics' and practitioners' blind spot – by championing Portia in the cause of feminism and focussing on Shylock to redress antisemitism, they were repeating the pattern of the hiring policies of the car manufacturing firm and leaving out Jessica. More significantly, they were also choosing to overlook how *both* Shylock's sexism and Portia's antisemitism are complicit in creating a world where the likes of Jessica are bound to fail one way or another. The play does not offer Jessica the same opportunities as Portia. Unlike the latter, whose cross-dressing affords her the prospect of sitting 'in her intelligence' without compromising her religion, a similar scenario does not exist for Jessica. Her cross-dressing leads to her liberation from patriarchy but at the cost of her religion.

As Angela Davis (1981) has repeatedly pointed out, especially in *Women, Race & Class*, if feminism is not only for the select few then gender equality cannot be theorized or practiced without committing to resistance against all forms of oppression, be it racial, religious, or economic because there are women belonging to all categories – Jews, Blacks, Muslims, disabled, poor – that are vulnerable to discrimination. The example of Jessica, explored through the framework of Black feminist theory, helped students to grasp that 'to look solely at hierarchies of gender defines the issue too narrowly and valorizes gender as the primary category of difference. Reading Portia as the heroic, subversive female proves particularly problematic when we place her actions in relation to other categories of difference' (Hall, 1992: 104). They were now able to answer their original question – 'can Portia be racist, antisemitic, and yet a feminist?' in the negative because they had recognized that to be racist and antisemitic is to contribute to the suppression of women of colour and women who are Jewish. However, they were also curious to discover how actresses had portrayed Jessica.

Records of such reflections are rare and not easily accessible, but we found audio clips in which Lilo Baur, who had played Jessica in the opening production of the play at Shakespeare's Globe, gives her insight into the role. In her informative article on the performance history of Jessica, Irene Middleton (2015) suggests that Baur's Jessica was completely accepted in Belmont in this production (307). Baur agrees with this assessment but she also draws attention to the text in which Jessica is called an 'infidel' (3.2.222) upon her first entry to Belmont and it serves to remind her that, even though converted, she is entering a society where she is an 'outsider'. She explains that 'we don't play it completely like this because Portia is open towards me because she looks more from the female [perspective?] like that Belmont is actually welcoming her in … she's not treated as an outsider but the text says she is an outsider … whatever we play the text says she is'.[54] It is revealing how Baur's reading of Jessica's nervousness in the face of the antisemitism directed at her was not allowed to fully manifest in this production in order to make Portia appear convivial from an ostensibly 'feminist' standpoint. Baur also insisted that she found 3.5 and the lines where Jessica praises Portia – 'It is very meet / The Lord Bassanio live an upright life, / For, having such a blessing in his lady, / He finds the joys of heaven here on earth' (3.5.70–73) – the 'most difficult' to play. She even

---

[54] Baur's interview is recorded as part of the 'Adopt an Actor' Series at Shakespeare's Globe and can be accessed here: https://soundcloud.com/the_globe/lilo-q05-1?in=the_globe/sets/adopt-an-actor-1998-the-merchant-of-venice-lilo-baur.

asks for suggestions on how to deliver these lines (Globe Education, 1998). My students pondered whether Jessica is trying to ingratiate herself to Portia's circle to fit in. They were led to this idea by Baur's claim that Jessica's betrayal of her father's intentions of wanting Antonio's flesh rather than his money is 'a way to be accepted in this society' which treats her with suspicion. The students wondered if Jessica praises Portia to align herself with Portia and her privileged status in this society. Finally, Baur insisted that Jessica remains uneasy in the play and her final line – 'I am never merry when I hear sweet music' (5.1.76) – indicates that she is 'troubled'.[55]

Baur's commentary led students to further questions about Jessica's silence in the final scenes. They found Middleton's article helpful in gleaning how in Loveday Ingram's 2001 production, Jessica 'demonstrated a deep sense of loss. During Belmont's music, she sat alone downstage, eventually breaking into Hebrew song and then choking tears' (Middleton, 2015: 306) or how, in Rebecca Gatward's 2007 production, she 'discarded her "Jewish" costuming in favour of "Christian" clothing and makeup. She also ate a bit of pork to prove her Christianity' (303). However, as students were now aware of the fissures and gaps that can exist between actresses' elucidations and the readings of their performances by others, they had a host of questions: did an actress playing Jessica agree with these critical observations? what parallels did an actress draw between her own life's realities and those of Jessica? what discussions did they have with their directors, male co-stars, and with actresses playing Portia? how did their experiences compare with Nerissa in the play and in performance who seems to be of a lower class than Portia? How did they decide to play their relationship to their religion? While the few accounts of Jessica invigorated debates in the classroom, students also realized that there are still huge critical gaps to be filled, especially in the case of characters like Jessica who are silent at key moments in the play.

Not every group might follow the shape of this discussion and another set of students with different backgrounds may not reach the same conclusions about Portia or Jessica or Nerissa. However, what is significant about recounting this experience is that contextualizing the play by focussing on actresses'

[55] https://soundcloud.com/the_globe/lilo-q05-1?in=the_globe/sets/adopt-an-actor-1998-the-merchant-of-venice-lilo-baur.

insights of the roles, whether the students agreed or disagreed with them, made them not only more astute readers of women characters in Shakespeare's plays but also helped them to place women both within the economic and socio-political world of the play and in the world outside the classroom. It also became clear that while rehearsal room experiences of actresses playing Portia had been helpful in looking at the gender dynamics of both the play and the performance, they also needed interviews from actresses (usually non-White and/or Jewish) who have performed the role of Jessica or from actresses who have played Nerissa if they were to grasp the 'intricately wrought nexus of anxieties over gender, race, religion, and economics' (Hall, 1992: 89) in the play, in rehearsal rooms, and by extension, in the world today.

2.2 Understanding Celia's Silences Through Actresses' Observations

Taking on board our findings after exploring *The Merchant of Venice*, we began our study of *As You Like It* by focussing on Celia, because just as Jessica is overshadowed by Portia in the former play, Celia is overlooked in the latter in comparison with Rosalind. Like Jessica, Celia is also silent in many moments in the play and (perhaps this is why) receives little space in production histories or scholarship. Commenting on the staging con-ditions of Shakespeare's time in which a boy actor would have played Celia, Scott McMillin (2004) conjectures that smaller and 'restricted' female roles (in which the character receives their cues from fewer cast members) might have been training parts for neophyte boy actors (231–45). Thus, for students reading the play, or criticism around it, Celia as an apprentice part does not register as an interesting or dynamic role. Interviews with modern directors (mostly male) further cement this impression. For instance, Michael Boyd confesses, 'I enjoyed the youth and frailty of Mariah Gale [who played Celia] in our production, which is repressed at court and covered with a determined optimism, then revealed as hopelessly out of depth in the forest'. In Boyd's interpretation, Celia is characterized by 'frailty' which only increases as the play progresses so much so that in the forest, she 'has to sit quietly and learn from Rosalind how to be ready for love when it strikes in the shape of Oliver' (Boyd,

2010: 155). Cusack, who played Celia in Terry Hands' 1980 production recounts how she was shocked to discover that the costume for Celia was green. When she challenged the director that, 'if I'm green and the set's green, I am going to disappear into the set', she was told, 'don't be so stupid, Sinead. You *are* the set' (quoted in Rutter, 1988: 115). For both Hands in 1980 and Boyd in 2009, Celia is a character who is meant to 'sit quietly and learn' or recede into the background to be forgotten.

Such interpretations are counterintuitive to actresses who have played the role, particularly because unlike Ophelia whose speech, as I argue in Section 1, is stifled under the patriarchal authority of her brother, father, and Hamlet, there is no ostensible reason for Celia's silence when she is in the forest, away from her father's court. Moreover, Celia cannot be 'hopelessly out of depth in the forest' as Boyd has suggested because 'it is Celia, not Rosalind, who proposes the journey in disguise to Arden' (Segal, 2008: 2). Fiona Shaw and Juliet Stevenson, who played Celia and Rosalind respectively in Adrian Noble's 1985 production of the play, do acknowledge that the 'major challenge' for the actress playing Celia is her 'silence' in the second half of the play (Shaw & Stevenson, 1988: 66). However, silence does not connote insignificance. Instead of being indicative of inexperience, the role might invite more input from the actress who must decide how to occupy these silences. Shaw and Stevenson explain that there are numerous ways to play Celia's relative 'silence', especially in 3.3 in which Rosalind, dressed as Ganymede, promises to cure Orlando of his love for Rosalind with some role-play. As Ganymede, (s)he suggests that if Orlando calls upon them at their cottage every day and woos him/her as 'Rosalind' then he shall be rid of his love 'madness' (3.3.331). As Rosalind/Ganymede and Orlando fix upon this plan, Celia is silent. However, the text indicates that she is present, so Shaw and Stevenson (1988) speculated:

> What *is* Celia's attitude to it all? Wonder, horror, amusement, rage, confusion, isolation, jubilation, fear, or all of these? How should she be placed physically on the set? Should she be at the side, like a spectator, or centrally, as a third character in the action? (66)

After considering and rehearsing several possibilities, they decided to layer 'many of the options at once'. They also discovered that as Ganymede 'Rosalind draws strongly on Celia's presence; to show off, outrage, seek refuge in, and silently confer with' (66, 66–7). Therefore, in this case, Stevenson and Shaw arrived at a performance that was in marked contrast to Boyd's or Hands' opinions and, by their technique of layering emotions, challenged McMillin's hypothesis about the role belonging to actors with less experience. Whereas the directors' interpretation of Celia was that it is a passive role, Stevenson and Shaw made Celia an active participant in the scene, someone who confers with Rosalind/Ganymede. In their version, it is the two cousins who are laying the 'snare' or 'prank' or 'love-test' or 'love education plan' for Orlando.

Paying attention to actresses' rehearsal and performance experiences provided a rich entry point to my students for studying Celia and for re-thinking the staging of this scene so they decided to enact it. In doing this, the students not only noticed how much of a team Celia and Rosalind are but also discovered that even when Celia is silent, she can build a great rapport with the audience. This was apparent when Kate, the student playing Celia, seemed to be dictating audience response. For instance, after Rosalind/Ganymede boasts to Celia that they are going to speak to Orlando as a 'saucy lackey' (3.3.250), Kate's Celia pushed Rosalind/Ganymede towards Orlando to encourage them to have a conversation. She then settled herself in a spot where she could see the couple and be seen by the audience. When Orlando looked at her at the beginning of the conversation, she pretended to be engrossed in reading. When Rosalind/Ganymede approached Orlando and asked the most mundane question 'what is't o' clock?' (3.3.253) only to get a cheeky reply from Orlando that there is 'no clock in the forest' (3.3.255), Kate's Celia tittered and so did the audience. When Rosalind/Ganymede suggested the audacious plan of their role-play, Kate's Celia's expressions changed from nervousness about their cover being blown to disbelief that the plan actually worked. In analysing their responses, the students agreed that Celia became an index to measure their own feelings and reactions to the scene. The students' experiential knowledge was confirmed by Sophie Thompson, who played Celia in

Geraldine McEwan's production of the play, because she writes that 'that Celia is a sort of mouthpiece for the audience as well, a representative up on stage, joining with them in watching what's going on' (Thompson, 1993: 78). Reading Thompson's reflection reinforced their own experience of the role and allowed the students to work on Celia's relationship with the audience throughout the play. They concluded that whereas Rosalind uses words in the form of asides, Celia uses a different visual language to build camaraderie with the audience.

The idea that Celia communicates differently was strengthened when students engaged with Nadia Nadarajah's interview on *Women & Shakespeare* which I had recorded specially to aid my teaching. Nadarajah performed Celia at Shakespeare's Globe in 2018 and 2019. Jenna Segal (2008) has argued that an approach to the play that takes into consideration race as well as gender would notice the subversive potential of Celia who, as she steps into the forest as Aliena, brings attention to instability of racial signifiers by deciding that she will 'with a kind of umber smirch [her] face' (1.3.102) to appear 'browner' (4.3.83). By casting a Brown Celia, this production raised questions not so much about racial 'performativity' as about 'contemporary criticism's neglect of Aliena's "browner" identity' (Segal, 2008: 10, 15). However, Nadarajah's casting also gave Celia a new language for her silences because she performed Celia in British Sign Language (BSL).[56] Glossing her Celia's silences, Nadarajah (2021) explained:

> I want you to think about my background as a deaf person and my community. It's very common, what happens. I am like Celia. You know how that she was walking around with Rosalind and Rosalind would be doing all the talking. That would be me with other people that could hear. We'd be alongside. We wouldn't be saying anything. We'd be mixing around with many people that could hear and there'd only be one deaf person in that community, if you like. Then somebody would be taking me along to somewhere and they

[56] The conversation with Nadia Nadarajah was interpreted by Linda Bruce.

would say, 'Oh, she's only deaf. She won't understand what
we're saying', so they could chat openly, and I'd just
observe people.

After providing a parallel between Celia's navigation through the play and
her embodied experiences in offstage life, Nadarajah elaborated that, in
this production, 'Celia was a representation of me in some way'. It is not
that Nadarajah (2021) decided to play Celia as deaf arbitrarily. Instead,
she stressed that it was 'relevant for [Celia] to be deaf' because this could
be an alternative explanation for Celia being present in so many scenes but
not having many spoken lines. Her recognition of Celia as potentially
a deaf role chimes with Siebers's theorization of disability as knowledge.
Section 1 used Siebers's formulation to understand Ophelia's connection
with mental disability. However, it is pertinent for comprehending Celia's
role in connection with physical disability too. Discussing Falstaff's
consternation on losing his horse in *Henry IV, Part 1* and noting that he
immediately starts measuring the distance he would now need to traverse
on foot, Siebers (2016) writes that 'those of us who notice that Falstaff is
disabled know it, and know it instantly, not because he shows biological
signs of a disability or withdraws from a disabling environment. We know
it because he embodies the knowledge of what it means to be a disabled
person. He calculates walking distances relative to an awareness of the
ground' (441). Similarly, although Celia is not explicitly deaf in the text,
Nadarajah's embodied knowledge of what it means to be deaf person
helped her to identify Celia's similar behaviour in the text and see her as
a deaf character.

H-Dirksen L. Bauman and Joseph J. Murray (2014) go further than
Siebers in reconceptualizing such embodied knowledge of aural disability as
'deaf gain'.[57] As opposed to 'hearing loss', the term 'deaf gain' refers to the
'unique cognitive, creative, and cultural gains manifested through deaf ways

[57] I would like to thank Susan Anderson who first drew my attention to deaf gain
and generously gave her time to discuss Nadarajah's podcast episode with me.
For more of her work on Shakespeare and Disability Studies, listen to her podcast
episode on *That Shakespeare Life* (Anderson, 2019).

of being in the world' (xv). Nadarajah's deaf gain enabled her to provide fresh interpretations of the text and ask probing questions for historical research by drawing analogies between herself and Celia. She questioned whether 'when Shakespeare wrote it, had he met a deaf person, had he used that person as a character' (Nadarajah, 2021)? Although this is an interesting research avenue, we do not need definitive proof that Shakespeare wrote Celia as a deaf character or that Celia was played by a deaf actor in Shakespeare's lifetime. As a play, the text welcomes new meanings with every performance, and *As You Like It* benefits from at least considering the performance possibilities of interpreting Celia as a deaf role. In the Shakespeare's Globe production, Celia's deafness elucidated the bond between the cousins. When Celia and Rosalind interacted with each other in this production, Celia would use BSL and Rosalind would speak and sign simultaneously thereby emphasizing both Rosalind's verbal and Celia's visual vernacular. Once the audience was used to concentrating on Celia's visual language, they became sensitive to Celia's gestures even when she had no lines. This dynamic had the effect of amplifying Celia's presence and further gave the impression that the cousins were a team and could communicate in a different language even with others around them. However, it also illustrated the ways in which Celia could feel marginalized at moments when Rosalind ignored her. Picking up on this, Kirwan (2018) writes that Nadarajah's 'Celia was a revelation; the noisiest Celia, in fact, that I've ever seen. Absolutely insistent that people attend to her (including stamping her feet when those she was speaking to rudely turned away)'. Nadarajah (2021) explained that when she interprets characters as deaf and 'other' in Shakespeare's plays, she plays them as assertive based on her embodied knowledge: 'I am a woman of colour. I'm deaf, I'm different to other people in society at the moment, so I have to be assertive and make sure that I have some equality, some standard with other people'. Elaborating on her gestural language she explained that deaf people 'are always waving their arms' but 'we are told to hold on and wait'.

Moreover, Celia's deafness unlocked scenes that other actresses have struggled with. For instance, in 1.2 when Orlando wins a wrestling match but is dismissed by Duke Fredrick for being the son of his enemy, Celia suggests that she and Rosalind should 'thank him and encourage him' (1.2.192) to make up for her father's rude behaviour. After performing Celia in McEwan's production, when Thompson (1993) played Rosalind in John Caird's production she found this scene 'difficult to do from a staging point of view' (79) because Celia is present when Rosalind and Orlando have a conversation and realize that they have fallen in love. In contrast, Nadarajah found the scene quite natural. According to her, Celia is on stage at this point because 'us deaf people' can 'see how people are behaving through their body language'. Nadarajah (2021) elaborates that her Celia registered Rosalind's attraction before Rosalind herself:

> Look at Rosalind in the play. She loved Orlando, didn't she? But she didn't realize initially, but she was flirting with him. Her eyes are fluttering. She was giggling. Now Celia could see that, she could see it. She couldn't hear what was being said, but she was watching their body language and she thought 'Oi'. And this is what deaf people are like.

My students noted that Nadarajah's reading of Celia fit particularly well with the text because Celia urges that Rosalind should accompany her in commending the youth and she says:

> Sir, you have well deserved,
> If you keep your promises in love
> But justly, as you have exceeded all promise,
> Your mistress shall be happy.
>
> (1.2.194–97)

This manner of congratulating somebody on winning a wrestling match might register as odd but Nadarajah's interpretation opens the performance possibility that Celia is talking about love at this point because she has already recognized the attraction between Rosalind and Orlando and is trying to steer the conversation in that direction. Paying attention to the way in which Nadarajah's intersectional experience enabled her to craft a unique Celia made my students appreciate why it was vital to record insights from diverse actresses who had played women characters that are frequently overlooked in Shakespeare scholarship. They recognized that such observations could open performance options for marginalized women characters in Shakespeare's plays – possibilities that they had not even thought were possible.

2.3 Podcasts as Cyberfeminist Archives

Baur's thoughts on playing Jessica are from the 'Ask an Actor' (formerly known as 'Adopt an Actor') initiative at Shakespeare's Globe. This extraordinary collection of interviews with the actors, actresses, and creative teams who have been a part of performances at this playhouse is being made available as audio playlists resembling a mini podcast series. Nadarajah's interview on playing Celia is from the *Women & Shakespeare* podcast. These examples demonstrate that the podcast format has already proved useful in disseminating insights from actresses who have played overlooked Shakespeare roles. One of the most obvious reasons for using podcasts to archive such material is that, like other digital or cyber archives, such as *Digital Theatre+*, *Drama Online*, and *Women Writers Online*,[58] they can both house media that has already been generated and facilitate the production of new and marginalized material before storing it for posterity. As there is a dearth of conversations with Shakespeare actresses, we can redress this lack through podcasts and then keep these interactions and conversations safe for the future. In this way, Shakespeare podcasts would resemble especially commissioned books in the field such as the 'Players of Shakespeare' series, or *Brutus and Other Heroines* (Walter, 2016), or *Performing Shakespeare's Women* (Reynolds, 2018), mentioned elsewhere in this section, in which Shakespeare actresses reflect on their performance choices in various roles. The key difference between these archives and podcasts is that the latter is attuned towards collecting and engendering verbal as opposed to written or filmed matter.[59] Even though actresses have

---

[58] See more about the project here: www.wwp.northeastern.edu/wwo/.

[59] The fact that podcasts can capture verbal diversity in terms of accents and voices is to be celebrated. Additionally, as Nadarajah's podcast interview in this chapter proves, verbal communication need not lead to the exclusion of deaf actresses of Shakespeare. While this fundamentally audio medium can appear inaccessible to

proved their interpretive acumen in their exquisite prose in written publications, podcasts might offer a more natural way of creating this material because asking actresses for reflections in an oral format might play to the strengths of performers who are already skilled at verbal communication rather than demanding that they master academic or even popular conventions of writing. Granted, there are also books such as the RSC editions or *The Arden Research Handbook of Shakespeare and Contemporary Performance* (Kirwan & Prince, 2021), discussed in the introduction to this section, and videos on digital platforms in which actresses are interviewed rather than required to write. However, podcasts might also have an advantage over these publication formats because the serial quality of the podcast allows a conversation to be released as soon as one episode is recorded rather than having to wait to reach a critical mass of interviews before publishing and audio recording is cheaper than filming. Moreover, the flexibility in the length of podcast episodes, which can range from a couple of minutes to full hours, also means that a conversation can be kept short and take place between rehearsal calls or can be detailed if time permits. Therefore, the format adapts to an actress' pattern of working. Thus, podcasts can be efficient ways to 'combat the inevitable silences and gaps in other archives' (Wakimoto, quoted in Sadler & Cox, 2018: 160) and create 'counter-memories' (Reitsamer, quoted in Sadler & Cox, 2018: 160) in Shakespeare performance literature. On the whole, podcasts offer an attractive solution for producing and collecting such interviews.

However, this technology is handy for storing and archiving too. Feminists have repeatedly stressed the importance of creating and preserving archives. Glasgow Women's Library in Scotland and the Feminist Library in London are two such initiatives that have recognized the value of rescuing

people who are deaf and hard of hearing, podcasters such as Miri Josephs (who considers herself a part of the deaf community) have insisted that podcasts are attractive to deaf people. While fully recognizing the ways in which the podverse currently sidelines the deaf community, I contend that rather than the rest of us deciding that podcasts are exclusionary, every podcaster can and should learn how to make their podcast more accessible to the deaf and hard of hearing from pioneers such as Josephs.

women from the dustbin of history by archiving documents of women's activism, their everyday lives, and achievements.[60] Unfortunately, archives such as these often struggle financially; London's Feminist Library has been forced to relocate several times due to rental increase. As an avid library user, I cannot overstate the value of such spaces, but an attraction of podcasts in this regard is that, in contrast to printed books or video, the sound format requires relatively little storage space so that a lot of material can be accommodated. However, as Wernimont, developing Ellen Rooney's ideas, has argued, an 'additive approach' (Rooney, 2006: 3) in which we simply pile up material or mere presence ('the fact of being archived somewhere') is 'not enough' (Wernimont, 2013) if the idea is to create archives that are feminist in both content and functionality. The archives need to be both accessible and usable since it is availability of material that dictates scholarship, lessons that can be taught, and historical narratives that can be written for future consumption. It is through their accessibility that podcasts reach their full potential as cyber-feminist archives because the contents are easy to retrieve. Dever, amongst others, has remarked that 'digital technologies have transformed archival access for researchers in ways that offer degrees of democratisation for what was once an elite practice available principally to the privileged few with time, money and credentials' (Dever, 2017: 1). Section 1 discussed the financial affordability of podcasts, but it is also worth noting that 'podcasts move with the human body' (Spinelli & Dann, 2019: 7). Instead of having to go to the physical archives, this aural archive not only comes to the listener through the RSS feed but can be taken on a journey. In fact, the most common ways to listen to a podcast are while commuting, walking, or engaging in other physical activities. So, even more than video or written digital media, podcasts do not require additional time commitments.

Making an observation regarding digital archives specifically, Dever voices a concern echoed by feminist archivists more generally that 'if archives matter for us as feminists, then their mattering is bound up in their productivity and potential far more than any idea of the past' (Dever,

---

[60] Find out more about the Glasgow Women's Library here: https://womenslibrary .org.uk/ and about the Feminist Library in London here: https://feministlibrary .co.uk/.

2017: 3). That is, it is important to register that the 'activist archives' such as the one I am advocating that we should create will only be feminist if they 'continue to be *activated* in the present and for the future' (Eichhorn, 2013: 160, original emphasis). Podcasts are relatively easy to share because they are 'interwoven into social media and as such have a heightened capacity to enhance engagement with, and activate, an audience. The same mobile devices used to participate in social media are the devices used to listen to (and in some cases produce) podcasts and there is ready and easy overlap between these uses' (Spinelli & Dann, 2019: 8). Besides social media, podcasts are also easy to embed into PowerPoint and virtual learning environments that are used for teaching so these are archives that can be introduced and discussed in the classroom and beyond with little effort or expertise. Therefore, podcasts are feminist in their affordances and would pay rich dividends if we, as educators, produce and use these in our curriculum or commit to a feminist podagogy in Shakespeare performance studies.

In 2007, using podcasting for the dual purpose of producing and archiving, Dayna McLeod said that 'we hope that our podcasts will reach audiences who need to hear queer voices, women's voices – and reflect a unique history. What we're learning through this podcasting project, is that if we don't archive our own queer culture, no one else will' (quoted in Hogan, 2008: 210). She seems to echo Barbara and Beverly Smith, who wrote in 1978 that 'as Black women, as lesbians and feminists, there is no guarantee that our lives will ever be looked at with the kind of respect given to certain people from other races, sexes, or classes . . . We must document ourselves now' (quoted in Gumbs, 2011: 17). If diverse actresses are being excluded from performance histories of Shakespeare, thereby foreclosing feminist readings of his plays in the present and future, then it is urgent that we record their voices now and share them with our students. Podcasts can come to our aid.

3 Feminist Shakespeare 'Podagogy' in Practice

The previous sections argued for developing and enacting feminist podagogy or participating in cyberfeminism by designing and utilizing podcasts for gender equity in Shakespeare Studies. These sections also demonstrated some of the basic ways in which podcasts can be used in the classroom to engage students with diverse women's voices in Shakespeare. This section takes a more practical approach and offers podcast-based activities and assignments to try out for making a Shakespeare course more gender inclusive. In his study of podagogies, Verma admits that it is often hard to obtain 'reflection by educators' about 'why they teach' with podcasts, 'what they have learned about it, and how they prepare syllabi and conduct classes'. He warns that '[w]ithout this perspective, collective wisdom about the practice, as well as details about the day-to-day work of assignments and assessments could be lost' (Verma, 2021: 143). While he addresses these lacunae by interviewing instructors who have taught various subjects through guiding their students in creating podcasts, I take a different route and sketch out activities and assignments for feminist podagogy. However, it is worth stressing that feminist podagogy is not meant to be merely a how-to or practical guide. Just like pedagogy, it is both a practice and involves taking an evaluative and analytical stance. In devising the pedagogical exercises below, some questions that have proved essential are: how can the use of podcasts in the classroom promote an engagement with feminist scholarship on Shakespeare? How can we employ podcasts to empower and activate women's voices in our classrooms? What might be some feminist uses of podcasts in the Shakespeare curriculum? To what extent can podcasts be utilized for feminist pedagogy in Shakespeare Studies? Are there meaningful ways in which cyberfeminism, Shakespeare, and teaching can interact? How can we train our students to use Shakespeare podcasts critically in the service of feminism?

As might be clear from these questions, feminist podagogy does not take an unquestionably congratulatory stance towards podcasts. As with any digital resource or educational tool, podcasts present a host of limitations and challenges. So, the aim of feminist podagogy is to foster a bidirectional relationship between feminism and podcasting in Shakespeare scholarship so that podcasts can nurture feminism in teaching but crucially, our feminist focus can also help identify the limitations of current Shakespeare podcasts and suggest ways in which these can be improved in order to function as feminist tools. To put it another way, podcasts can aid in making our course feminist but our concentration on feminism might teach us how to 'hack' Shakespeare podcasts for feminist use or provide Shakespeare podcasters with suggestions and ideas to make their design and content feminist. Through feminist podagogy, the digital tool of podcasts can thus be taught to shape itself for feminist Shakespeare classrooms.

The plans that follow are intended to be roadmaps for teachers. Therefore, each begins with an 'Overview' which contextualizes the assignments and activities and helps to clarify the practical and conceptual aims. The 'Learning Outcomes' can be shared with students so that they can appreciate the point of the assignments and assess whether they have achieved the desired objectives. These are followed by step-by-step 'Activity' suggestions that combine critical discussions, workshop-style creations, and research. The 'Selected Resources' in the next segment are the ones that I have used repeatedly in my classroom but they can be easily adapted to align with different courses. As each of these plans has been road-tested in my Shakespeare courses, the 'Student Responses' give a snapshot of the ways in which these exercises were received. The students' feedback on podagogy maps future directions for a feminist Shakespeare pedagogy. In addition, it paves the way for Shakespeare podcasts to respond to feminist needs in the curriculum.[61]

3.1 Diversifying Citational Practices

Overview

Section 1 established that our students' perception of who is considered an authority in Shakespeare Studies is influenced by who is represented in academic conferences and public lectures. Therefore, the bias against the public voice of women that reverberates across Shakespeare's time and ours, in Shakespeare's texts and in our discipline, produces a bias in identifying the experts that students cite in their academic work. Discussing 'sexism and

---

[61] I want to thank Sarah Olive for generously devoting her time and expertise, and brainstorming some ways in which podcasts can be incorporated into classroom activities. I have developed plans 3.1 and 3.3 based on her suggestions. For more such ideas, listen to Olive (2021) in a podcast episode recorded by *Women & Shakespeare* in collaboration with the British Shakespeare Association.

racism in citational practice', Ahmed (2017) asserts that we need to pay attention to citations because these are like 'academic bricks through which we create houses. When citational practices become habits, bricks become walls' (148). In other words, failure to chip away at sexism and racism in speaking invitations and citational practices is akin to creating hard 'brick walls' for women and women of colour in the field thereby robbing it of rich polyvocal scholarship. Ahmed's remedy is 'to create a crisis around citation, even just a hesitation, a wondering that might help us not to follow well-trodden citational paths' (148). In the first section, I asserted that Shakespeare podcasts can make us rethink who we want to hear from in public and academic discourse because these podcasts model more inclusive spaces and this, in turn, can generate a hesitation and crisis around speaker invitations and citation practices. However, instead of a top-down stance in which we wait for our research culture to become diverse and trickle down to the students, we can take a two-pronged approach and train our students to seek diversity in deciding who to cite in their academic work. This exercise uses podcasts to help students to first identify their own (often unconscious) bias while selecting authoritative voices to listen to and cite, and then supports them to correct this bias, reflect on why it needs rectifying, and finally curate a polyvocal research resource for themselves and for their peers.

Learning Outcomes

Students will:

1. examine their own unconscious bias in choosing experts
2. reflect on how critical dialogue can be enriched by including multiple viewpoints
3. use podcasts for curating a multivocal research resource

Activity

– Divide students into groups and task them with curating a research resource on any Shakespeare play or topic. This resource should take the form of a playlist of ten episodes from the multitude of Shakespeare podcasts online. These playlists should feature experts who can be cited in essays. Avoid giving them a topic such as 'women and Shakespeare' because the idea is to examine whether they include a diverse range of women scholars in the playlists even when the prompt does not explicitly signal the need to do so. Introduce students to a selection of Shakespeare podcasts but assure them that they are not limited to these series only.

– Once they have a playlist, discuss why they chose those experts and how they decided that the speakers in these episodes were authorities who could be cited.

– Now, encourage them to identify at least one way in which they can make their playlist feminist, whether it is by including women as the subject of discussion within a particular theme or by incorporating more women speakers in their playlist, or extending the diversity of speakers in terms of race, age, class, ability, and professions. Discuss why it might be important to include voices of women in their playlists. Mary Beard's 'The Public Voice of Women' (2014) is a helpful starting point because it outlines the marginalization of women's public voices.

– Collectively listen to the revised playlists and analyse what the newly included experts brought to their research resource. This is an important step because it makes students engage with the advantages of diversity and steers them away from tokenism in their inclusions.

– Ask them to reflect on how the activity changed their perspectives on who they could cite in their scholarship.

Selected Resources

– Beard, M. (2014). 'The Public Voice of Women'.
– Some Shakespeare podcasts that might be particularly useful for this exercise are *Shakespeare Unlimited*, *Such Stuff*, *Women & Shakespeare*, and *That Shakespeare Life* because these feature guests and critics in every episode.

Student Responses

My students were asked to design an audio research resource on *Hamlet*. When they curated their first playlists and compared notes, they were surprised by how similar their playlists were despite working independently. They reflected that they had nominated experts based on scholars' previous citations or celebrity status of the artists. Perhaps owing to the nature of the resources that they drew upon, the students' playlists were gender balanced but each group enjoyed the challenge of diversifying their playlists further and reflecting on what this added to their scholarship. For instance, one group revised their playlist to make space for two episodes: one in which Deanne Williams (2016) talks about Ophelia and girlhood and another in which an actor of colour Shubham Saraf (2018) talks about playing Ophelia. They pointed out that the speakers and their scholarship added to their understanding of Ophelia as a complex and nuanced character. However, they noted that ultimately their playlists were limited by who has been already recorded. For instance, students could not find episodes that featured research on Gertrude. They concluded that although podcasts were more inclusive in their guests than academic conferences, there is further scope for diversifying the speakers on these podcasts.

3.2 Recording Underrepresented Knowledges

Overview

In Section 1, I suggested that podcasts can be used to amplify the voices of women scholars who are not given an equal platform in public discourse and academic conferences. In Section 2, I argued that conversations with a diverse range of actresses who have played frequently overlooked Shakespeare roles can be a significant asset in studying Shakespeare's plays and that podcasts can be employed in building such an archive of insights. However, it is not only actresses or scholars who have a monopoly on Shakespeare knowledge. For instance, as Natasha Korda's archival research has demonstrated, women's backstage contributions to 'the purportedly all-male professional stage' of Shakespeare's time have not been fully considered. Her book argues that:

> the rise of the professional stage relied on the labor, wares, ingenuity, and capital of women of all stripes, including

ordinary crafts- and tradeswomen who supplied costumes,
props, and comestibles; wealthy heiresses and widows who
provided much-needed capital and credit; wives, daughters,
and widows of theater people who worked actively alongside their male kin; and immigrant women who fuelled the
fashion-driven stage with a range of newfangled skills and
commodities.

(Korda, 2011: 1)

In a different vein, Katherine Schiel (2012) has shown how women, including
women of colour, formed clubs and read Shakespeare in the late nineteenth
century and thus had a hand in shaping the sociocultural legacy of the
playwright. Korda's and Schiel's recovery work is valuable for showing us,
among other things, the kinds of artistic, financial, and intellectual labour of
women that is disregarded when we study Shakespeare. Korda's and Schiel's
research was made possible due to surviving archives and their study of these
materials has been germinal to our understanding of women's contributions
to Shakespeare theatre and Shakespeare criticism. Therefore, it is incumbent
upon us to document Shakespeare knowledges from a range of women
besides scholars and actresses in order to enable current and future work of
this kind. Since it is now widely understood that 'rather than a destination for
knowledges already produced or a place to recover histories and ideas placed
under erasure, the making of archives is frequently where knowledge production begins' (Eichhorn, 2013: 3), podcasts are useful as they can aid in both
producing and storing such information. Due to the ease of recording and
publishing, podcasts are also a faster way to fill the gaps in our information.
This seminar activity will encourage students to reflect upon which professions get left out in Shakespeare scholarship and how podcasts can be a way to
redress the situation.

Learning Outcomes

Students will:

1. exhibit an understanding of different stakeholders who participate in
   Shakespeare scholarship, theatre, and cultural production

2. discover women's 'hidden' contributions to Shakespeare
3. reflect on the ways in which podcasts can broaden the pool of voices that are given the opportunity to comment on Shakespeare and aid in the creation of an archive for future study

Activity

– Divide students into three groups. Group 1 should research everyone involved in creating a Shakespeare performance for stage, screen, or audio platforms. Extracts from Korda's work can aid this group in their thinking because she talks about roles such as propmakers, financiers, and costume designers. Although her work is historicist, her sustained attention to the different kinds of production labour might inspire students to investigate backstage roles more thoroughly. Group 2 has the task of finding out all personnel who lend their expertise in creating a Shakespeare book, a journal, or a database. Listening to *Shakespeare Unlimited* podcast episode 44 which includes interviews with archivist and conservation specialists Renate Mesmer and Austin Plann-Curley (2016) might be interesting to this group. Group 3's responsibility is to think about all the other ways in which Shakespeare gets lodged into our culture and the people who facilitate that embeddedness. Scheil's work might force them to cast their net widely when they dwell on people beyond academia, publishing, and theatre.

– Once the groups have conducted their research, ask them to share which professions remain underrepresented in scholarly and public Shakespeare conversation.

– All the groups should now research if women are represented in these overlooked categories. If yes, they should identify women whom they would invite as a guest if they were using a podcast to bridge gaps in our learning.

– Finally, discuss whether their perception of women's contributions to Shakespeare altered as a result of gathering this information and whether their understanding of Shakespeare changed.

Selected Resources

- Scheil, K. (2012). *She Hath Been Reading*.
- Korda, N. (2011). *Labors Lost: Women's Work and the Early Modern English Stage*.
- Mesmer, R., & Plann-Curley, A. in conversation with Grant, N. (2016). Ep. 44. www.folger.edu/shakespeare-unlimited/conservation-lab.

Student Responses

Students identified several kinds of expertise that did not commonly feature in discussions about Shakespeare. They were surprised that archivists, who are so crucial to research, were often not included in discussions about Shakespeare. Their findings chime with critics such as Kate Eichhorn (2013) who has noted that academic conferences have often 'reinforced the idea that archives and special collections exist simply to serve scholars' research mandates or to house scholars' own papers' (2) or with Michelle Caswell (2016) who writes that '[e]ven those whose work focuses on gender and class' have been 'blind to the intellectual contributions and labor of [the archival field] that has been construed as predominantly female, professional (that is, not academic), and service-oriented, and as such, unworthy of engagement'. Students also recognized that cartoonists, marketing personnel, prop makers, and fight directors would all make good podcast guests and add to our knowledge. They found that women were represented in these professions. The fight and intimacy director, Yarit Dor, was one of the people they said they would like to hear from so *Women & Shakespeare* recorded a podcast episode with her (Dor, 2022). Students also agreed that their conception of Shakespeare changed as they realized how much collective endeavour and often unseen labour of women goes into maintaining Shakespeare as a cultural force.

3.3 Pitching Your Own Podcast

Overview

Our students are immersed in Web 2.0 which requires them to contribute to public information and knowledge flows from tweets and gifs to blogs and videos. Increasingly Shakespeare educators bring Web 2.0 tools into their classrooms both as sources of information and to boost their students' critical participation in this online culture. They have designed assignments in which students create blogs, videos, and wikis either alongside or as an alternative to the traditional essays and presentations. To take just two examples from the many, O'Neill (2014) suggests encouraging students to make a YouTube video 'as part of [their] response to Shakespeare'. This, he adds, could be 'the mashup, the video-essay, the movie-trailer parody' or their own adaptation which gives them a chance to 'experiment with form, plot, character and language' (218). Katheryn Giglio and John Venecek designed an assignment in which their pupils combined text and media to create wikis about social identities in Shakespeare's plays. These scholars propose a learn-by-doing approach with technology because they contend that sharing their research and analysis publicly would help students to 'find their voices as scholars fully engaged in the act of knowledge production' (Giglio & Venecek, 2009) and others add that it would also foster a critical attitude towards this practice as they navigate and 'reflect on the diversity of contemporary knowledge-making methods' (Kill, 2012: 404). As early as the 1990s, Pramaggiore and Hardin (1999), among others, sought to investigate whether this technological pedagogical methodology 'can support and enhance the feminist classroom' (164). They conducted their test with a listserv and webpage to which students contributed, and concluded that digital technologies not only *could* be used to 'enact a feminist pedagogy' (172) but *should* be used for feminist pedagogy. They quote Jennifer Terry and Melodie Calvert and agree with their conclusions that to 'refuse such an engagement is perhaps not merely to forgo the strategic opportunity to transform or even invent radically different technologies for feminist and progressive projects' but rather 'crucial decision-making about our futures required this critical engagement' (quoted in Pramaggiore & Hardin, 1999: 172). In this, Hardin and Pramaggiore echo the cyberfeminist call both to critique the cyberspace for its gender oppression and to engage with cyber technologies to 'hack' them for feminist use (Sajbrfem, 2008). Building on these studies within the fields of Shakespeare, feminist pedagogy, and cyberfeminism which advocate an active involvement in the technosphere on the one hand and joining in the trend of Podagogy 2.0 in which educators guide students to build their own podcasts (Verma, 2021) on the other, this assignment is an opportunity for students to move beyond consuming or evaluating Shakespeare. It invites them to pitch their own podcast series which can contribute to public knowledge of feminist Shakespeares.

Learning Outcomes

Students will:

1. familiarise themselves with feminist Shakespeares
2. discover and analyse cyberfeminism or feminist uses of technology
3. take steps towards creating public feminist Shakespeare knowledge in the digital space through podcasts

Activity

- Invite students to suggest ideas for a Shakespeare podcast that is feminist in its orientation. They can pitch ideas for an episode, a mini-series, or an entire podcast. They should familiarize themselves with existing Shakespeare podcasts before airing their ideas.
- Discuss myriad feminist approaches to Shakespeare. This is a diverse and vast area of scholarship. The 'Selected Resources' section lists some books that I have used in the past. However, bear in mind that neither of these books contain essays that explicitly address the interconnections of technology, feminism, and Shakespeare because work in this area is just beginning.
- Introduce students to cyberfeminism to enumerate examples of the ways in which technology can be harnessed for feminist use. Again, the 'Selected Resources' section gives a few suggestions that might be useful. I have found that looking at instances of cyberfeminist work motivates students to think subversively and playfully about the podcast content and format.
- Once students have had time to develop their ideas, discuss their pitches in the seminar and, if the format of the course permits, encourage them to realize their ideas and record a pilot episode for their podcast.

Selected Resources

- Some books that I have used to give students of a sense of urgent debates and discussions around feminist approaches to Shakespeare are *A Feminist*

Companion to Shakespeare (Callaghan, 2016), *Shakespeare and Feminist Theory* (Novy, 2017), *Things of Darkness: Economies of Race and Gender in Early Modern England* (Hall, 1995) and *Shakespeare, Race and Performance* (Jarrett-Macauley, 2017).

– In terms of resources for cyberfeminism, for the advanced readers, *Cyberfeminism 2.0* (Gajjala & Oh, 2012) is both incisive and inspiring. For beginners, I assign Sajbrfem's accessible lecture slides, 'Cyberfeminism 101' (Sajbrfem, 2008) which outlines the history or rather the 'herstory' of the field and offers some ways in which students can engage with cyberfeminism. In the seminars, we have also seen some examples of cyberfeminist work such as *Conceiving Ada* – a film which revolves around a fictional modern day computer scientist, Emmy Coer, who finds a way to communicate with Ada Lovelace, a historical figure who was author of the first computer algorithm – or we have discussed 'Cyberfeminism 100 Anti-Theses', which is a playful art manifesto and seeks to provide an anti-definition of cyberfeminism.[62] Although not labelled as cyberfeminism, it might also be useful for students to browse the range of projects and discussions in *Bodies of Information: Intersectional Feminism and the Digital Humanities* (Losh & Wernimont, 2019).

Student Responses

Students thoroughly enjoyed this activity and proposed striking and original podcast ideas. One of the students pitched a mini-series which would focus only on women characters in Shakespeare, such as Paulina and Jessica, who are silent but present in different scenes in the play. Her first episode, which she recorded, concentrated on the scene from the end of *The Winter's Tale* when Leontes suddenly decides to marry Paulina off to Camillo and she does not have any lines. The student asked her classmates to imagine vocal responses from Paulina on hearing this declaration. Some of the recorded responses included sighing, mocking laughter, and a scream. Another episode that she had planned would announce that it presents Jessica's dialogue from the final scene of *The*

---

[62] https://conversations.e-flux.com/t/feminist-art-manifestos-100-anti-theses-on-cyberfeminism/1846.

Merchant of Venice and would be a recording of ten minutes of silence with voices in the distance to emphasize that Jessica has no lines at the end of the play. A different student was inspired by *Conceiving Ada* and Germaine Greer's *Shakespeare's Wife* (Greer, 2007), and suggested a review show called 'what would Anne Hathaway say?' This podcast series would adopt the persona of Shakespeare's wife and critique Shakespeare's plays from her perspective. A third student suggested the idea of enlarging the geographical boundaries of feminist criticism in Shakespeare. She wanted to create a series which would take advantage of her dual heritage and include interviews with Japanese actresses who have performed in Shakespeare's plays. This podcast would be bilingual and have episodes in Japanese and English.

3.4 Forging Communities

Overview

On Twitter, #ShakeRace is used by scholars of colour to share resources, provide support, and exchange research and pedagogical techniques on Critical Race Theory and Shakespeare. Like many others, Kirwan uses Twitter when he teaches his advanced module Screen Shakespeares: 'using the hashtag #Shaxfilm, students are invited to tweet their responses to the set film for the week, to share links with one another to further resources and websites and to pass around reactions'. He notes that what students are 'surprised and delighted by' is the discovery that there is 'a virtual community of other Shakespeare film enthusiasts wanting to engage with the debates being carried out in the live classes'. He elaborates that his students appreciated being 'part of a live and ongoing conversation across the world' (Kirwan, 2014a: 106). Therefore, for Shakespeare students, these online communities become a way to tap into larger networks of aficionados and experts where they can teach, learn, find opportunities, or share laughs over common interests. In contrast to such community building, listening to podcasts is usually a solitary activity. Spinelli and Dann refer to it as 'orphaned media' because it is 'delivered asynchronously and consumed individually' and it 'draws the listener away from others' (2019: 46). Yet, paradoxically, podcasts engender strong loyalties and are considered by many a community-building exercise. For instance, after using podcasts for their online course, Sara Archard and Rosina Merry (2010) reported that 'although we used a range of other technologies to help build a sense of community, we found that as the conversational podcasts developed, they began to form the metaphoric "glue" that holds the programme together' (5–6). While Spinelli and Dann (2019) concentrate on community building as a way to inculcate fandom that can be translated into financial gains when listeners buy tickets for live events and merchandise sales, they agree that it is rare to make money from podcasting. Most podcasters use their medium to start conversations on topics and interests that are ignored by mainstream broadcast media. The *Rice at Home* podcaster observes that many people 'don't have the people around them to have these conversations with, so they use the podcast as a medium to access these conversations and feel connected' (quoted in Vrikki & Malik, 2019: 279). Sarah Florini's (2015) research also supports this claim as it explores how Black US podcasters conceive of their podcasts as being akin to 'historically significant Black social spaces like barber/beauty shops and churches' (210). As Ahmed and Bailey, Jackson, and Welles assert, communities are a feminist essential. Ahmed (2017) includes 'other killjoys', as she terms feminists, in her 'survival toolkit' because 'the experience of having others who recognize the dynamics because they too have been there' (244) can provide solidarity, sustenance and energy. Bailey, Jackson, and Welles (2020) insist on the importance of digital communities for resisting misogynoir or anti-Black misogyny. This assignment turns from creators and hosts of the podcast to concentrate on the listeners and helps students to work through the ways in which podcasts can be deployed to build inclusive Shakespeare communities.

Learning Outcomes

Students will be able to:

1. work on feminist principles of community building
2. brainstorm ways in which Shakespeare podcasts can nurture communities
3. reflect on the ways in which such digital enclaves can be more inclusive

Activity

— Ask students, in groups, to discuss ways in which Shakespeare podcasts can nurture communities and facilitate listener participation. Spinelli and Dann's chapter and Florini's research can give them some ideas, as can researching existing podcasts with a huge fanbase. Encourage students to think beyond social media and urge them to suggest ideas that take advantage of the unique affordances of the podcast medium. For instance, as the podcast is aural and can therefore be a mobile medium, they could suggest a podcast walking club in which participants pick a meeting point, listen to the same podcast episode on their headphones while walking to the destination, and discuss the episode when they arrive.

— Once they have assembled their ideas, discuss ways in which the communities around podcasts can be more inclusive. Listening to *Women & Shakespeare* podcast episode with deaf actor Nadia Nadarajah (2021) will assist students in thinking about some of the ways in which podcasts can be more accessible both for speakers and listeners.

Selected Resources

— Nadarajah, N. in conversation with Panjwani, V. (2021). Series 2, Ep. 3. http://womenandshakespeare.com/.

— Florini, S. (2015). The podcast "Chitlin' Circuit": Black Podcasters, Alternative Media, and Audio Enclaves.

— Spinelli, M., & Dann, L. (2019). Chapter 3: You Are Not Alone: Podcast Communities, Audiences, and *Welcome to the Night Vale*.

Student Responses

Students suggested many ways to foster communities by widening listener participation. They argued that podcasts should aim for a two-way communication. Some of their ideas included the listeners sending questions and/or answers to the podcast hosts, creators encouraging comments and feedback, and organising listening parties in which participants listen remotely at different locations and chat about the episode via social media. Students were especially concerned about making podcasts more accessible and suggested that podcasters could produce better notes in the space provided for show-notes on podcasting platforms, provide links to resources mentioned in their podcasts, and include episode transcripts to enable the deaf community to participate in this new media. They also provided a trenchant critique of the anglocentric nature of both the Internet and Shakespeare and urged that, as a first step, podcast transcripts could be translated in different languages to make them open to non-English-speaking populations. At a simpler level, they argued that attaching better keywords or 'tags' to a podcast episode can lead to people making hitherto unnoticed associations. For example, they pointed out that tagging Nadarajah's episode with keywords such as 'deaf actors', 'feminist', and 'global Shakespeare' might invite people and scholars who had not realized that they had overlapping interests to attend to the podcast episode and interact with other listeners thereby diversifying their respective communities.

Conclusion: Press Play

This Element began by proposing that a podcast is a room in cyberspace, but such a virtual space is not intended to be understood as escapism from the gender inequities of the offline world. Rather, as the activism of cyberfeminists has proved, the online sphere is an opportunity to restructure or resist marginalization in the offline world. Wendy Harcourt (1999), Jessie Daniels (2009), Dorothy Kim (2018), and Saskia Sassen (2002) have stressed that online digital tools are embedded in the offline world. According to Sassen (2002), there is nothing like a 'purely digital' or 'virtual' space (366). Instead, as Harcourt (1999) writes, digital technologies are ways for 'creating a communicative space that when embedded in a political reality can be an empowering mechanism for women' (219). Karim-Cooper's and Lennon's testimonies or my students' frustrations with the soundscape of Shakespeare Studies signal the ongoing need for empowering methodologies for women in Shakespeare pedagogy. This Element suggests that one such praxis is feminist podagogy or using podcasts for shaping a more gender equitable Shakespeare Studies. Section 1 traced how this reshaping is already underway with numerous women producing and appearing as expert guests on Shakespeare podcasts that can be used in classroom teaching. As the section further outlined, this development is in marked contrast to the prejudice against the public voice of women which can be noted in the texts of Western classical antiquity, in instruction and pedagogical manuals of Shakespeare's time, in Shakespeare's plays such as *Hamlet* and *The Winter's Tale*, and in current academic and public conferences in Shakespeare Studies which have disproportionately platformed men as keynote speakers. Section 2 urged that podcasts can become activist archives of the kind that are advocated by feminists who have shown the importance of recording overlooked histories of women. In Shakespeare Studies, podcasts can be used as archival spaces for collating the insights of Shakespeare actresses as this knowledge can help students and scholars in considering a wide range of performance possibilities of women's roles in Shakespeare's plays, particularly overlooked roles such as Jessica in *The Merchant of Venice* or Celia in *As You Like It*. Through suggested lesson plans such as 'Recording Underrepresented Knowledges', 'Diversifying Citational Practices', 'Pitching Your Own Podcast', and 'Forging Communities', Section 3 further proved that the virtual amplifying, archiving, and community building that podcasts can facilitate will alter who our students consider to be the experts in the field, who they study, who they cite, which characters they analyse, what lens they adopt, and even how they engage with Shakespeare. We can conclude that there is a complex mutuality or symbiotic relationship between embodied reality and cyberspace where hegemonies and activisms in one arena can produce a change in the other. As the gender and racial hierarchies oppress or press upon us in our material world, we can play in cyberspace to transform and present alternative realities. Conversely, we can also press back on online gender oppressions by utilizing the activist scholarship developed in our discipline through the ages. This Element thinks about how to use podcasts for this dual action in Shakespeare pedagogy. It advocates a feminist podagogy in Shakespeare Studies.

Press Play.

References

ACMRS Arizona. (2020). It's Time to End the Publishing Gatekeeping!: A letter from RaceB4Race Executive Board, *The Sundial*, https://medium.com/the-sundial-acmrs/its-time-to-end-the-publishing-gatekeeping-75207525f587.

Aebischer, P. (1999). 'Yet I'll speak': Silencing the Female Voice in *Titus Andronicus* and *Othello*. *Actes des congrès de la Société française Shakespeare*, 17, 27–46.

Ahmed, S. (2017). *Living a Feminist Life*. Croydon: Duke University Press.

Amnesty International. (2017). *Toxic Twitter*. www.amnesty.org/en/latest/research/2018/03/online-violence-against-women-chapter-1/.

Anderson, S. in conversation with Cassidy, C. (2019). Susan Anderson on Disability in Shakespeare's England. *That Shakespeare Life* [Podcast], Ep. 76. www.cassidycash.com/ep-76-susan-anderson-on-disability-in-shakespeares-england/.

Archard, S., & Merry, R. (2010). Podcasts as a Conversational Pedagogy. *Computers in New Zealand Schools: Learning, leading, Technology*, 22(3), 1–11.

Battershill, C., & Ross, S. (2017). *Using Digital Humanities in the Classroom: A Practical Introduction for Teachers, Lecturers, and Students*. London: Bloomsbury.

Bauman, H.-D. L., & Murray, J. J. (2014). Deaf Gain: An Introduction. In H.-D. L. Bauman & J. J. Murray, eds., *Deaf Gain: Raising the Stakes for Human Diversity*. Minneapolis: University of Minnesota Press, pp. xv–xlii.

Beard, M. (2014). The Public Voice of Women. *London Review of Books*, 36(6), 11–14.

Belton, E. (2000). Speech in Dumbness: Female Eloquence and Male Authority in *The Winter's Tale*. In J. K. Rodeheffer, D. Sokolowski & J. S. Lee, eds.,

Core Texts in Conversation. New York: University Press of America, pp. 157–63.

Benjamin, R. (2017). But . . . There Are New Suns!. *Palimpsest: A Journal on Women, Gender, and the Black International*, 6(1), 103–5.

Benjamin, R. (2019). *Race after Technology: Abolitionist Tools for the New Jim Code*. Cambridge: Polity Press.

Boose, L. E. (1991). Scolding Brides and Bridling Scolds: Taming the Woman's Unruly Member. *Shakespeare Quarterly*, 42(2), 179–213.

Boyd, M. interviewed by J. Bate and K. Wright (2010). The Director's Cut: Interviews with Dominic Cooke and Michael Boyd. In J. Bate & E. Rasmussen, eds., *As You Like It*. London: Macmillan, pp. 144–56.

Brockbank, P. (1989). Introduction: Abstracts and Brief Chronicles. In P. Broackbank, ed. *Players of Shakespeare 1: Essays in Shakespearean Performance by Twelve Players with the Royal Shakespeare Company*. Cambridge: Cambridge University Press, pp. 1–10.

Brown, D. S. (2021). (Early) Modern Literature: Crossing the 'Sonic Color Line'. *Shakespeare, Race & Pedagogy* [Conference Talk]. www.shakera cepedagogy.com/.

Brown, K., & Kirwan, P. (2010). *The Merchant of Venice* in Performance: The RSC and Beyond. In J. Bate and E. Rasmussen, eds., *The Merchant of Venice*. London: Macmillan, pp. 114–39.

Brown, K., & Sewell, J. (2010). *As You Like It* in Performance: The RSC and Beyond. In J. Bate & E. Rasmussen, eds., *As You Like It*. London: Macmillan, pp. 113–43.

Callaghan, D. (ed.). (2016). *A Feminist Companion to Shakespeare*. New Jersey: John Wiley & Sons.

Carson, C., & Kirwan, P. (eds.). (2014). *Shakespeare and the Digital World: Redefining Scholarship and Practice*. Cambridge: Cambridge University Press.

Caswell, M. L. (2016). "The Archive" Is Not an Archives: On Acknowledging the Intellectual Contributions of Archival Studies. *Reconstruction: Studies in Contemporary Culture*, 16 (1), https://escholarship.org/uc/item/7bn4v1fk.

Ciston, S. (2019). ladymouth: Anti-Social-Media Art As Research. *Ada: A Journal of Gender, New Media, and Technology*, 15, https://doi.org/10.5399/uo/ada.2019.15.5.

Cole, T. (2012). The White-Savior Industrial Complex. *The Atlantic*, www.theatlantic.com/international/archive/2012/03/the-white-savior-industrial-complex/254843/.

Coles, K., Hall, K., & Thompson, A. (n.d.). BlacKKKShakespearean: A Call to Action for Medieval and Early Modern Studies. *MLA Profession*, https://profession.mla.org/blackkkshakespearean-a-call-to-action-for-medieval-and-early-modern-studies/.

Crenshaw, K. (2016). *The Urgency of Intersectionality*. TED Talk, www.ted.com/talks/kimberle_crenshaw_the_urgency_of_intersectionality?language=en.

Croll, D. in conversation with Panjwani, V. (2020). Doña Croll on Cleopatra, John of Gaunt, Black Actors in Britain. *Women & Shakespeare* [Podcast], Series 1, Ep. 2, http://womenandshakespeare.com/.

Cusack, S. (1989). Portia in *The Merchant of Venice*. In P. Broackbank, ed. *Players of Shakespeare 1: Essays in Shakespearean Performance by Twelve Players with the Royal Shakespeare Company*. Cambridge: Cambridge University Press, pp. 29–40.

Daniels, J. (2009). Rethinking Cyberfeminism (s): Race, Gender, and Embodiment. *Women's Studies Quarterly*, 37(1/2), 101–24.

Das, N., & Price, E. in conversation with Lennon, W. (2021). *Shakespeare, Race & Pedagogy* [Conference Session]. www.shakeracepedagogy.com/.

Davis, A. Y. (1981). *Women, Race, & Class*. New York: Random House.

Dever, M. (2017). Archives and New Modes of Feminist Research. *Australian Feminist Studies*, 32 (91–2), 1–4.

Dor, Y. in conversation with Panjwani, V. (2022). Yarit Dor on Fighting and Intimacy on the Shakespeare Stage in *Hamlet*, *As You Like It*, and *Romeo & Juliet*. *Women & Shakespeare* [Podcast], Series 3, Ep. 3, http://womenand shakespeare.com/.

Döring, N., & Mohseni, M. R. (2019). Male Dominance and Sexism on YouTube: Results of Three Content Analyses. *Feminist Media Studies*, 19(4), 512–24.

Edison Research & Triton Digital. (2019). *She Listens: Insights on Women Podcast Listeners*. www.edisonresearch.com/wp-content/uploads/2019/10/She-Podcasts-2019.pdf.

Edison Research & Triton Digital. (2020). *The Infinite Dial 2020*. www.edisonresearch.com/wp-content/uploads/2020/03/The-Infinite-Dial-2020-U.S.-Edison-Research.pdf.

Eichhorn, K. (2013). *The Archival Turn in Feminism: Outrage in Order*. Philadelphia: Temple University Press.

Findlay, D. (1993). Portia in *The Merchant of Venice*. In R. Jackson & R. Smallwood, eds., *Players of Shakespeare 3: Further Essays in Shakespearean Performance by Players with the Royal Shakespeare Company*. Cambridge: Cambridge University Press, pp. 52–67.

Fischer, S. K. (1990). Hearing Ophelia: Gender and Tragic Discourse in *Hamlet*. *Renaissance and Reformation/Renaissance et Réforme*, 14(1), 1–10.

Florini, S. (2015). The Podcast "Chitlin' Circuit": Black Podcasters, Alternative Media, and Audio Enclaves. *Journal of Radio & Audio Media*, 22(2), 209–19.

Forcepoint. (n.d.). What is a Firewall?: Firewalls Defined, Explained, and Explored. *Cyber Edu*, www.forcepoint.com/cyber-edu/firewall.

Friedman, M. D. (2002). *The World Must Be Peopled: Shakespeare's Comedies of Forgiveness*. London: Associated University Press.

Friend, C. (2016). Winona Ryder and the Internet of Things. *Hybrid Pedagogy*, https://hybridpedagogy.org/winona-ryder-internet-things/.

Frizzell, N. (2016). 'I felt like morse tapping his first code' – the Man who Invented the Podcast. *The Guardian*, www.theguardian.com/tv-and-radio/2016/nov/03/christopher-lydon-podcast-inventor-open-source-mp3-files-interview.

Gajjala, R. (2003). South Asian Digital Diasporas and Cyberfeminist Webs: Negotiating Globalization, Nation, Gender, and Information Technology Design. *Contemporary South Asia*, 12(1), 41–56.

Gajjala, R., & Oh, Y. J. (eds.). (2012). *Cyberfeminism 2.0*. New York: Peter Lang.

Gay, P. (2002). Portia Performs: Playing the Role in the Twentieth-Century English Theatre. In J. W. Mahon & E. M. Mahon, eds., *The Merchant of Venice: New Critical Essays*. London: Routledge, pp. 431–54.

Giglio, K., & Venecek, J. (2009). The Radical Historicity of Everything: Exploring Shakespearean Identity with Web 2.0. *Digital Humanities Quarterly*, 3 (3), http://digitalhumanities.org:8081/dhq/vol/3/3/000063/000063.html.

Glitch & The End Violence Against Women Coalition. (2020). *The Ripple Effect: COVID-19 and the Epidemic of Online Abuse*, https://glitchcharity.co.uk/wp-content/uploads/2021/04/Glitch-The-Ripple-Effect-Report-COVID-19-online-abuse.pdf.

Globe Education. (1998). *Lilo Baur: Activities* [Activity Sheet for Schools]. Adopt an Actor (GB 3316 SGT/ED/LRN/2/1/4). The Shakespeare Globe Trust, London.

Greer, G. (2007). *Shakespeare's Wife*. New York: Bloomsbury.

Gumbs, A. P. (2011). Seek the Roots: An Immersive and Interactive Archive of Black Feminist Practice. *Feminist Collections: A Quarterly of Women's Studies Resources*, 32(1), 17–21.

Hall, K. F. (1992). Guess Who's Coming to Dinner? Colonization and Miscegenation in *The Merchant of Venice*. *Renaissance Drama*, 23, 87–111.

Hall, K. F. (1995). *Things of Darkness: Economies of Race and Gender in Early Modern England*. London: Cornell University Press.

Harcourt, W. (1999). Conclusion: Local/Global Encounters: WoN Weaving Together the Virtual and Actual. In W. Harcourt, ed. *Women@ Internet: Creating New Cultures in Cyberspace*. London: Zed Books, p. 219.

Henderson, D., & Vitale, K. S. (eds.). (2022). *Shakespeare and Digital Pedagogy: Case Studies and Strategies*. London: Bloomsbury.

Henderson, D. E. (2006). The Artistic Process: Learning from Campbell Scott's *Hamlet*. In D. Henderson, ed. *A Concise Companion to Shakespeare on Screen*. Oxford: Blackwell, pp. 77–95.

HESA. (2021). *Higher Education Staff Data: What Areas Do They Work In?* www.hesa.ac.uk/data-and-analysis/staff/areas.

Hirsch, B. (2012). *Digital Humanities Pedagogy: Practices, Principles and Politics*. Open Book. www.openbookpublishers.com/books/10.11647/obp.0024.

Hogan, M. (2008). Dykes on Mykes: Podcasting and the Activist Archive. *Topia: Canadian Journal of Cultural Studies*, 20, 199–215.

Jackson, S. J., Bailey, M., & Welles, B. F. (2020). *# HashtagActivism: Networks of Race and Gender Justice*. London: MIT Press.

Jarrett-Macauley, D. (ed.) (2017). *Shakespeare, Race and Performance: The Diverse Bard*. London: Routledge.

Jarrett-Macauley, D. in conversation with Panjwani, V. (2020). Delia Jarrett-Macauley on *Moses, Citizen & Me, Shakespeare, Race and Performance*. *Women & Shakespeare* [Podcast], Series 1, Ep. 1. http://womenandshakespeare.com/.

Juhasz, A. (2014). Conclusion: It's Our Collective, Principled Making That Matters Most: Queer Feminist Media Praxis@ *Ada*. *Ada: A Journal of*

Gender, New Media, and Technology, 5, https://doi.org/10.7264/N3610XMD.

Kai, M. (2019). 'There Is Rhythm in the Language': Actress Christiana Clark Finds the 'Jazz' in Shakespeare in *The Winter's Tale*. *The Root*, www.theroot.com/there-is-rhythm-in-the-language-actress-christiana-cla-1834875286.

Kamaralli, A. (2007). Female Characters on the Jacobean Stage Defying Type: When is a Shrew Not a Shrew?. *Literature Compass*, 4(4), 1122–32.

Karim-Cooper, F. in conversation with Panjwani, V. (2020). Farah-Karim Cooper on Shakespeare's Globe, Sam Wanamaker Playhouse, Cosmetics, Gestures. *Women & Shakespeare* [Podcast], Series 1, Ep. 4, http://womenandshakespeare.com/.

Kill, M. (2012). Teaching Digital Rhetoric: Wikipedia, Collaboration, and the Politics of Free Knowledge. In B. Hirsch, ed., *Digital Humanities Pedagogy: Practices, Principles and Politics*. Open Book, pp. 389–405.

Kim, D. (2018). How to #DecolonizeDH: Actionable Steps for an Antifascist DH. In D. Kim & J. Stommel, eds., *Disrupting the Digital Humanities*. Punctum Books, pp. 479–93.

Kim, D., & Stommel, J. (eds.). (2018). *Disrupting the Digital Humanities*. Punctum Books.

Kimbro, D., Noschka, M., & Way, G. (2019). Lend Us Your Earbuds: Shakespeare/ Podcasting/ Poesis. *Humanities*, 8(2), 67, https://doi.org/10.3390/h8020067.

Kirwan, P. (2014a). 'From the table of my memory': Blogging Shakespeare in/out of the Classroom. In C. Carson & P. Kirwan, eds., *Shakespeare and the Digital World: Redefining Scholarship and Practice*. Cambridge: Cambridge University Press, pp. 100–12.

Kirwan, P. (2014b). Introduction: Pedagogy. In C. Carson & P. Kirwan, eds., *Shakespeare and the Digital World: Redefining Scholarship and Practice*. Cambridge: Cambridge University Press, pp. 58–62.

Kirwan, P. (2018). *As You Like It* @ Shakespeare's Globe. *The Bardathon* [Blog], https://blogs.nottingham.ac.uk/bardathon/2018/07/01/like-shakespeares-globe/.

Kirwan, P., & Prince, K. (eds.). (2021). *The Arden Research Handbook of Shakespeare and Contemporary Performance*. London: Bloomsbury Publishing.

Korda, N. (2011). *Labors Lost: Women's Work and the Early Modern English Stage*. Philadelphia: University of Pennsylvania Press.

Kothari, A. (2021). Women & Shakespeare Podcast. *Teaching Shakespeare*, 20, 5–7.

Lennon, W. (2021). Shakespeare, Race & Pedagogy. *Teaching Shakespeare*, 21, 4–7.

Losh, E., & Wernimont, J. (eds.). (2019). *Bodies of Information: Intersectional Feminism and the Digital Humanities*. Minneapolis: University of Minnesota Press.

Luiggi, C. M. (2016). 'She May Strew Dangerous Conjectures': The Political Sedition and Social Potency of *Hamlet*'s Ophelia. *Selected Papers of the Ohio Valley Shakespeare Conference*, 9(1), 77–86.

McKay, A. (2000). Speaking Up: Voice Amplification and Women's Struggle for Public Expression. In C. Mitchell, ed., *Women and Radio: Airing Differences*. New York: Routledge, pp. 15–28.

McMillin, S. (2004). The Sharer and His Boy: Rehearsing Shakespeare's Women. In P. Holland & S. Orgel, eds., *From Script to Stage in Early Modern England*. Basingstoke: Palgrave, pp. 231–45.

Mesmer, R., & Plann-Curley, A. in conversation with Grant, N. (2016). 'To Repair Should Be Thy Chief Desire'. *Shakespeare Unlimited* [Podcast], Ep. 44. www.folger.edu/shakespeare-unlimited/conservation-lab.

Middleton, I. (2015). A Jew's Daughter and a Christian's Wife: Performing Jessica's Multiplicity in *The Merchant of Venice*. *Shakespeare Bulletin*, 33 (2), 293–317.

Moberly, D. C. (2018). 'Once more to the breach!': Shakespeare, Wikipedia's Gender Gap, and the Online, Digital Elite. In S. O'Neill, ed., *Broadcast Your Shakespeare: Continuity and Change Across Media*. London: Bloomsbury, pp. 87–104.

Mond, F. (1910 quoted 2015). Letter to Israel Gollancz, Secretary of the British Academy quoted in Frida Mond: A Good friend to the British Academy. *British Academy Review*, 25, 52–5.

Mottram, C. (2016). Finding a Pitch that Resonates: An Examination of Gender and Vocal Authority in Podcasting. *Voice and Speech Review*, 10(1), 53–69.

Mulready, C. (2022). Shakespeare Students as Scribes: Documenting the Classroom through Collaborative Digital Note-taking. In D. E. Henderson & K. S. Vitale, eds., *Shakespeare and Digital Pedagogy: Case Studies and Strategies*. London: Bloomsbury, pp. 13–24.

Nadarajah, N. in conversation with Panjwani, V. (2021). Nadia Nadarajah on Shakespeare in Sign Language (BSL), Celia, Titania, Guildenstern, Cleopatra. *Women & Shakespeare* [Podcast], Series 2, Ep. 3, http:// womenandshakespeare.com/.

Ng-Gagneux, E. (2022). Reading Interculturality in Class: Contexualising and Studying Global Shakespeares in/through A|S|I|A. In D. E. Henderson & K. S. Vitale, eds., *Shakespeare and Digital Pedagogy: Case Studies and Strategies*. London: Bloomsbury, pp. 89–103.

Novy, M. (2017). *Shakespeare and Feminist Theory*. London: Bloomsbury.

Olive, S. (2015). *Shakespeare Valued: Education Policy and Pedagogy 1989–2009*. Chicago: Intellect Books.

Olive, S. in conversation with Panjwani, V. (2021). Sarah Olive on Shakespeare in Education. *Women & Shakespeare* [Podcast], Series 3, Ep. 1, http://womenandshakespeare.com/.

O'Neill, S. (2014). *Shakespeare and YouTube: New Media Forms of the Bard*. London: Bloomsbury.

Pogson, K. in conversation with Panjwani, V. (2020). Kathryn Pogson on Portia, Ophelia, Lady Anne. *Women & Shakespeare* [Podcast], Series 1, Ep. 5, http://womenandshakespeare.com/.

Pramaggiore, M., & Hardin, B. (1999). Webbed Women: Information Technology in the Introduction to Women's Studies Classroom. In B. Winkler & C. DiPalma, eds., *Teaching Introduction to Women's Studies: Expectations and Strategies*. London: Bergin & Garvey, pp. 163–73.

RAJAR. (2018). *MIDAS Winter 2018*. www.rajar.co.uk/docs/news/MIDAS_Winter_2018.pdf.

RAJAR. (2020). *MIDAS Spring 2020*. www.rajar.co.uk/docs/news/MIDAS_Spring_2020.pdf.

Refskou, A. S. (2021). Introduction: Representing Richard: Shakespeare, Otherness and Diversity in Global Settings. *Otherness: Essays and Studies*, 8(2). www.otherness.dk/journal/otherness-essays-studies-82/.

Reynolds, P. M. (2018). *Performing Shakespeare's Women: Playing Dead*. London: Bloomsbury.

Richards, J., & Thorne, A. (2007). Introduction. In J. Richards & A. Thorne, eds., *Rhetoric, Women and Politics in Early Modern England*. New York: Routledge, pp. 1–24.

Richards, R. S. (2011). 'I Could Have Told You That Wouldn't Work': Cyberfeminist Pedagogy in Action. *Feminist Teacher*, 22 (1), 5–22.

Richardson, S., & Green, H. (2018). Talking Women/Women Talking: the Feminist Potential of Podcasting for Modernist Studies. *Feminist Modernist Studies*, 1(3), 282–93.

Rogers, J. (2022). The British Black and Asian Shakespeare Performance Database: Reclaiming Theatre History. In D. E. Henderson & K. S. Vitale, eds., *Shakespeare and Digital Pedagogy: Case Studies and Strategies*. London: Bloomsbury, pp. 78–88.

Rooney, E. (2006). Introduction. In E. Rooney, ed., *The Cambridge Companion to Feminist Literary Theory*. Cambridge: Cambridge University Press, pp. 1–10.

Rosenberg, M. (1992). *The Masks of Hamlet*. London: University of Delaware Press.

Ross, S. C., & Smith, R. (2020). Beyond Ovid: Early Modern Women's Complaint. In S. C. Ross & R. Smith, eds., *Early Modern Women's Complaint: Gender, Form, and Politics*. Cham: Palgrave, pp. 1–26.

Rutter, C. (1988). *Clamorous Voices: Shakespeare's Women Today*. London: Women's Press.

Sadler, R., & Cox, A. M. (2018). 'Civil disobedience' in the Archive: Documenting Women's Activism and Experience through the Sheffield Feminist Archive. *Archives and Records*, 39(2), 158–73.

sajbrfem (2008). *Cyberfeminism 101*, https://www.slideshare.net/sajbrfem/cyberfeminism-101.

Sample, I. (2020) Internet 'is not working for women and girls', says Berners-Lee: *The Guardian*, www.theguardian.com/global/2020/mar/12/internet-not-working-women-girls-tim-berners-lee.

Saraf, S. in conversation with Greenberg, I. (2018). The Ensemble Experiment. *Such Stuff* [Podcast], Series 1, Ep. 3.

Sassen, S. (2002). Towards a Sociology of Information Technology. *Current Sociology*, 50(3), 365–88.

Scheil, K. W. (2012). *She Hath Been Reading: Women and Shakespeare Clubs in America*. New York: Cornell University Press.

Segal, J. (2008). 'And browner than her brother': 'Misprized' Celia's Racial Identity and Transversality in *As You Like It*. *Shakespeare*, 4(1), 1–21.

Shakespeare, W. (1999). *Hamlet*. R. Hapgood, ed., Cambridge: Cambridge University Press.

Shakespeare, W. (2002). *Hamlet*. C. Watts, ed. Hertfordshire: Wordsworth Editions.

Shakespeare, W. (2006a). *Hamlet*. A. Thompson and N. Taylor, eds., London: Bloomsbury.

Shakespeare, W. (2006b). *Hamlet: The Texts of 1603 and 1623*. A. Thompson and N. Taylor, eds., London: Bloomsbury.

Shakespeare, W. (2007). *The Winter's Tale*. S. Snyder and D. T. Curren-Aquino, eds. New York: Cambridge University Press.

Shakespeare, W. (2009). *As You Like It*. M. Hattaway, ed. Cambridge: Cambridge University Press.

Shakespeare, W. (2010). *The Merchant of Venice*. J. Bate and E. Rasmussen, eds. London: Macmillan.

Shaw, F., & Stevenson, J. (1988). Celia and Rosalind in *As You Like It*. In P. Brockbank, R. Jackson & R. Smallwood, eds., *Players of Shakespeare 2: Further Essays in Shakespearean Performance by Players with the Royal Shakespeare Company*. Cambridge: Cambridge University Press, pp. 55–72.

Sher, A. interviewed by J. Bate and K. Wright (2010). Playing Shylock: Interviews with Antony Sher and Henry Goodman. In J. Bate and E. Rasmussen, eds., *The Merchant of Venice*. London: Macmillan, pp. 156–74.

Siebers, T. (2016). Shakespeare Differently Disabled. In V. Traub, ed., *The Oxford Handbook of Shakespeare and Embodiment: Gender, Sexuality, and Race*. Oxford: Oxford University Press, pp. 435–54.

Smith, K. (2017). *Gender, Speech, and Audience Reception in Early Modern England*. New York: Routledge.

Spender, D. (1981). The Gatekeepers: A Feminist Critique of Academic Publishing. In H. Roberts, ed., *Doing Feminist Research*. London: Routledge, pp. 186–202.

Spinelli, M., & Dann, L. (2019). *Podcasting: The Audio Media Revolution*. New York: Bloomsbury.

Stallybrass, P. (1986). Patriarchal Territories: The Body Enclosed. In M. Ferguson, M. Quilligan & N. Vickers, eds., *Rewriting the*

Renaissance: The Discourses of Sexual Difference in Early Modern Europe. Chicago: University of Chicago Press, pp. 123–42.

Sterne, J., Morris, J., Baker, M. B., & Freire, A. M. (2008). The Politics of Podcasting. *The Fibreculture Journal*, 13, https://thirteen.fibreculturejournal.org/fcj-087-the-politics-of-podcasting/.

Stommel, J. (2014). Critical Digital Pedagogy: A Definition. *Hybrid Pedagogy*, https://hybridpedagogy.org/critical-digital-pedagogy-definition/.

Sullivan, E. (2014). Internal and External Shakespeare: Constructing the Twenty-First-Century Classroom. In C. Carson & P. Kirwan, eds., *Shakespeare and the Digital World: Redefining Scholarship and Practice.* Cambridge: Cambridge University Press, pp. 63–74.

Thompson, S. (1993). Rosalind (and Celia) in *As You Like It.* In R. Jackson & R. Smallwood, eds., *Players of Shakespeare 3: Further Essays in Shakespearean Performance by Players with the Royal Shakespeare Company.* Cambridge: Cambridge University Press, pp. 77–86.

Tiku, N., & Newton, C. (2015). Twitter CEO: 'We suck at dealing with abuse': Dick Costolo says Trolls are Costing Twitter Users. *The Verge.* www.theverge.com/2015/2/4/7982099/twitter-ceo-sent-memo-taking-personal-responsibility-for-the

Verma, N. (2021). Sound and Pedagogy: Taking Podcasting into the Classroom. In M. Bull & M. Cobussen, eds., *The Bloomsbury Handbook of Sonic Methodologies.* New York: Bloomsbury Academic, pp. 140–54.

Vives, J. L. (c.1528). *Instruction of a Christen Woman.* R. Hyrde, trans. London.

Vrikki, P., & Malik, S. (2019). Voicing Lived-experience and Anti-racism: Podcasting as a Space at the Margins for Subaltern Counterpublics. *Popular Communication*, 17(4), 273–87.

Walter, H. (2016). *Brutus and Other Heroines: Playing Shakespeare's Roles for Women.* London: Nick Hern Books.

Warren, R. (1986). Shakespeare in Britain, 1985. *Shakespeare Quarterly*, 37 (1), 114–20.

Watters, A. (2014). Men Explain Technology to Me: On Gender, Ed-Tech, and the Refusal to Be Silent. *Hack Education*, http://hackeducation.com/2014/11/18/gender-and-ed-tech.

Waugh, D. (1656). *The Lambs Defence Against Lyes*. London: Giles Calvert.

Wernimont, J. (2013). Whence Feminism? Assessing Feminist Interventions in Digital Literary Archives. *DHQ: Digital Humanities Quarterly*, 7(1). www.digitalhumanities.org/dhq/vol/7/1/000156/000156.html.

Wernimont, J. (2015). No More Excuses [Blog], https://jwernimont.wordpress.com/category/toofew/.

Williams, D. (2012). Enter Ofelia Playing on a Lute. In K. Peterson and D. Williams, eds., *The Afterlife of Ophelia*. New York: Palgrave, pp. 119–36.

Williams, D. in conversation with Grant, N. (2016). 'Why, Here's a Girl!'. *Shakespeare Unlimited* [Podcast], Ep. 60. www.folger.edu/shakespeare-unlimited/girlhood.

Williams, N. (2016). *The Taming of the Shrew*, *Cymbeline*, and the World Shakespeare Congress. *Notinourstars* [Blog], https://notinourstars.wordpress.com/2016/08/09/the-taming-of-the-shrew-cymbeline-and-the-world-shakespeare-congress/.

Wittek, S., & McInnis, D. (eds.) (2021). *Shakespeare and Virtual Reality*. Cambridge: Cambridge University Press.

Woolf, V. (1929). *A Room of One's Own*. London: Hogarth Press.

Acknowledgements

I am deeply grateful to the 'Shakespeare and Pedagogy' series editors for their patience and thoroughness, and to the anonymous reviewer for such encouraging comments. Many thanks to those friends, colleagues, and family members who have both allowed me to discuss and present parts of this Element as well as held my hand through really dark times; Chirag Panjwani, Rajkumar Panjwani, Prerna Valecha, Amritesh Singh, Anne Sophie Refskou, Chloe Preedy, Delia Jarett-Macauley, Natasha Bell, Rachel Willie, you are all brilliant people. Megabytes of gratitude is also owed to my Zoom writing group who provided accountability checks each weekend and made completion possible. This Element is dedicated to my mum, Sushma Panjwani, to all my students, and my fellow women Shakespeare podcasters and educators because this Element would not have existed without you – I am in awe of you.

Cambridge Elements ≡

Elements in Shakespeare and Pedagogy

Liam E. Semler
University of Sydney

Liam E. Semler is Professor of Early Modern Literature in the Department of English at the University of Sydney. He is author of *Teaching Shakespeare and Marlowe: Learning versus the System* (2013) and co-editor (with Kate Flaherty and Penny Gay) of *Teaching Shakespeare beyond the Centre: Australasian Perspectives* (2013). He is editor of Coriolanus: A Critical Reader (2021) and co-editor (with Claire Hansen and Jackie Manuel) of Reimagining Shakespeare Education: Teaching and Learning through Collaboration (Cambridge, forthcoming). His most recent book outside Shakespeare studies is *The Early Modern Grotesque: English Sources and Documents 1500–1700* (2019). Liam leads the Better Strangers project which hosts the open-access Shakespeare Reloaded website (shakespearereloaded.edu.au).

Gillian Woods
Birkbeck College, University of London

Gillian Woods is Reader in Renaissance Literature and Theatre at Birkbeck College, University of London. She is the author of *Shakespeare's Unreformed Fictions* (2013; joint winner of Shakespeare's Globe Book Award), *Romeo and Juliet: A Reader's Guide to Essential Criticism* (2012), and numerous articles about Renaissance drama. She is the co-editor (with Sarah Dustagheer) of *Stage Directions and Shakespearean Theatre* (2018). She is currently working on a new edition of

A Midsummer Night's Dream for Cambridge University Press,
as well as a Leverhulme-funded monograph about Renaissance
Theatricalities. As founding director of the Shakespeare
Teachers' Conversations, she runs a seminar series that
brings together university academics, school teachers and
educationalists from non-traditional sectors, and she regularly
runs workshops for schools.

ABOUT THE SERIES

The teaching and learning of Shakespeare around the world is
complex and changing. *Elements in Shakespeare and Pedagogy*
synthesises theory and practice, including provocative, original
pieces of research, as well as dynamic, practical engagements with
learning contexts.

Elements in Shakespeare and Pedagogy

Lightning Source UK Ltd.
Milton Keynes UK
UKHW021247061222
413360UK00026B/423

9 781108 977180